SINGI

Singing to the Lord

D. Martyn Lloyd-Jones

BRYNTIRION PRESS

ISBN 1 85049 194 1

Cover design:
Evangelical Press, Darlington

Unless otherwise stated, all Scripture quotations are from
the Authorised (King James) version.

Published by Bryntirion Press
Bryntirion, Bridgend CF31 4DX, Wales, UK
Printed by Creative Print & Design, Ebbw Vale

Contents

1
Spirit-filled worship

*'And be not drunk with wine, wherein is excess; but be
filled with the Spirit; speaking to yourselves in psalms
and hymns and spiritual songs, singing and making
melody in your heart to the Lord; giving thanks
always for all things unto God and the Father
in the name of our Lord Jesus Christ.'*
(Ephesians 5:18-20)

In verse 18 of Ephesians chapter 5, the apostle has been
reminding us of the fundamental doctrine that as Christian
people we should be controlled in every part of our beings by the
Holy Spirit, and that we should keep on being filled with the
Spirit. In this, the Christian stands out in marked contrast to the
non-Christian. The Christian is someone who can be filled with
the Spirit of God, and that can only happen to a Christian.

In chapters 4, 5 and 6 of Ephesians, the apostle is concerned
to apply the doctrine that he laid down in the first three chapters
of this epistle. And in verse 19 of chapter 5 his purpose is to show
the practical outworking of the teaching in verse 18. If Christians
are to be filled and controlled by the Holy Spirit, how then does
this manifest itself in daily life and living?

The apostle starts with the way the Spirit is manifested when
Christian people meet together in church. Now you may well ask
why Paul begins here. And it seems to me that the answer is fairly
obvious. In laying down his doctrine about being filled with the
Spirit, in contrast to being drunk—filled or soaked—with wine,

Paul is very naturally thinking of the joyful, happy aspect of the Christian life. That immediately leads him to think of one way in which that happiness and joy manifest themselves—that is, in the realm of the church—and so he takes that up.

Expressing joy

I suggest that the apostle still has in mind the contrast he has drawn in verse 18. He is saying to these people: You remember what you used to do? You used to say to your friends, 'We'll meet together on such and such an evening and have a good time.' There would be the alcohol, the wine; you would start drinking, and that would loosen your tongues. Some would talk a lot, others would tell stories, and others would begin to sing. They would sing their ribald and bacchanalian songs, and you would all think you were having a marvellous time and enjoying yourselves to your hearts' content. That used to be your idea of happiness and conviviality.

But now, says Paul, I have already reminded you that as Christians you are not filled with wine but with the Holy Spirit. It therefore follows of necessity that your way of spending a happy evening with your fellow Christians will be very different. I will now remind you, says Paul, of the way in which you as Christians—filled with the Spirit of God—express your happiness, your joy. I will remind you of how you have a convivial time together, filled with the spirit of praise, rejoicing and thanksgiving.

Now that is the setting for this statement, and I am emphasising it because some people seem to think that in this verse the apostle is once and for ever laying down a church order from which no Christian may ever deviate. They regard his words almost as a legal enactment prescribing the order of church worship. I think it is quite clear from the context alone that that is not the case.

But there is also another reason, which is that the apostle is obviously only dealing with one aspect of what happens in church. He does not say a word here about preaching or prophesying; he does not say a word about teaching, or about many other subjects examined elsewhere in this epistle and in his other letters. So to approach this verse with a kind of legalistic attitude, as if the apostle is giving a final ruling on how praise is to be conducted in the church, is to miss the whole context, the whole atmosphere, of the apostle's teaching in this great section. He is concerned here about the way in which men and women show that they are filled with the Spirit when they are having fellowship together in their communal services of worship.

Now to me this is a very important and fascinating subject. Unfortunately, it has often become a matter of controversy, particularly with regard to the singing of psalms, and the great point of this passage has been entirely missed. So we must approach this verse with care. Very good people have gone wrong here, people whom one greatly respects and admires—and there are still such people. And therefore it behoves us to try to understand the apostle's exact teaching. To do so, we take, first of all, the actual phrases used by Paul.

'Speaking to yourselves'

Now clearly we must not be misled by this word 'speaking'. The Greek word does not refer only to speech; it really means using the voice, and you use your voice in singing as much as in speaking. It was a word that was used for the sounds made by animals, and for the sound made by a musical instrument. So Paul is not saying, 'First, this is how you must speak to one another, and then later comes singing and making melody in your hearts.' No, no; the whole verse refers primarily to singing.

Then the words 'to yourselves' are also a wrong translation. The Greek means 'among yourselves', 'to each other', 'to one another'. In other words, Paul is saying, 'You must give expression among yourselves to your happy, joyous emotions.' That is the idea he is conveying.

Now the authorities have been much exercised here as to whether Paul is referring to a particular form of singing—antiphonal or responsive singing—in which the minister (or leader) and the congregation sing alternate lines. Some have detected that here. Well, you cannot say that it is not here, and yet you are not fully entitled to say that it is. There is evidence to show that there was something like antiphonal singing in the early church, and it continues to be practised today in many sections of the church. But that is not the important issue. I repeat that the apostle is not laying down minute, particular regulations with regard to church worship, but is concerned that there should be combined singing: an expression of joy and happiness in the Lord. Filled with the Spirit, the people are now going to give voice to their praise.

It is, of course, well known that from the beginning singing was a definite part of Christian worship. The instructions for musicians and singers that are found in the psalms indicate that singing and the playing of musical instruments was a vital part of the worship of Israel, and the church began, after all, among the Jews. But music-making was not confined to the Jews. It is characteristic of most people that when they are full of joy, they have a desire to sing. So the practice of singing persisted into the Christian church.

'In psalms and hymns and spiritual songs'

Now it is here that controversy has arisen, and, admittedly, it is a very difficult matter. There are those who say that the words 'psalms', 'hymns' and 'spiritual songs' mean exactly the same thing and that the apostle is simply repeating himself for the sake of emphasis. They point out that in the book of Psalms, some psalms are referred to as 'songs'. They also point out that individual psalms are sometimes called 'hymns'. In the account of our Lord in the upper room with the disciples, for example, we read, 'And when they had sung an hymn' (Matthew 26:30), and that is undoubtedly a reference to a psalm.

So there are those who have always argued that the phrase 'psalms and hymns and spiritual songs' is a generic term to cover psalms, and means the whole of the book of Psalms. They say that Paul is telling the Christians in Ephesus to sing from the book of Psalms, and is ruling that nothing should ever be sung in the church save the psalms, and perhaps certain scriptural phrases or paraphrases. That point of view has been held by many in the church throughout the centuries, and is still held in a few places in the Christian church today.

But it is generally agreed by well-known writers on Ephesians, including scholars such as Charles Hodge and Eadie, and indeed by practically all the great commentators of the last two hundred years, that the words have different meanings. They hold that though the distinctions between them must not be pressed too far, the apostle mentions the three terms quite deliberately in order to give a general description of the wide variety of ways in which people filled with the Spirit give expression to their joy and happiness.

Psalms
The Hebrew word for 'psalm' is derived from a word meaning 'plucking the strings', and the authorities are generally agreed that the word means 'a sacred song designed to be sung to the accompaniment of a musical instrument'. So—and this is interesting in and of itself—this word came to be used for the particular form of sacred poem that is found in the book of Psalms, where the poems were almost invariably sung to the accompaniment of instrumental music such as the harp and lute.

11

Now it is possible that when Paul talks of 'psalms' in verse 19, he is actually referring to the book of Psalms, but it is also possible that he is not. I do not know. Men and women filled with the Spirit can write and compose psalms, they can write sacred poems in the style of the psalms.

Hymns

Now a hymn is essentially a song of praise to God, a divine song, a sacred, poetical composition. The great St Augustine gave a definition of a hymn. He said that a hymn must be praise of God, and it must be sung. And that has always been the generally accepted connotation of the word.

Now there are many who say that you get indications of such hymns in the New Testament. We are told, for instance—and I have no doubt that this is right—that certain compositions of this character were taught to the first Christians. It is very difficult for us to realise this because we are accustomed to having hymn books. But they did not, and many could not read. And so they were taught hymns. It is said that 1 Timothy 3:16 was probably a fragment of a hymn:

> *Without controversy great is the mystery of godliness:*
> *God was manifest in the flesh,*
> *justified in the Spirit,*
> *seen of angels,*
> *preached unto the Gentiles,*
> *believed on in the world,*
> *received up into glory.*

And it is not at all difficult to imagine that one section of the church sang, 'God was manifest in the flesh'; another section then sang, 'justified in the Spirit'; then another, 'seen of angels'; another, 'preached unto the Gentiles'; another, 'believed on in

12

the world'; and then that all together they sang, 'received up into glory'. This may well be a fragment of a hymn. What is clear is that in the early church the Christians certainly did sing such hymns.

Spiritual songs

A song is an ode, a lyric, and it is an interesting point that the apostle says '*spiritual* songs'. He does not need to say 'spiritual psalms' because by definition a psalm is a sacred song. Nor does he say 'spiritual hymns' because, as St Augustine reminds us, any hymn must not only be praise, it must be praise to God. And, of course, we still use the same kind of terminology when we talk about a hymn or psalm. There is no need to add that it is spiritual or sacred; that is taken for granted. But you can have all kinds of songs, secular as well as religious; you can have a comic song, for example. So the apostle has to qualify his statement: you must sing *spiritual* songs.

Now what does Paul mean by 'spiritual songs'? He is talking to people who are filled with the Spirit—that is the context of this verse. So a spiritual song must be the sort of song that is inspired by the Spirit; it must be the composition of someone who is spiritual, and it must be about spiritual matters. Odes and lyrics can be written about all sorts of things, but the apostle is emphasising that his readers are to have only odes or lyrics that are on spiritual themes. Of necessity, their songs will be totally unlike the songs they used to sing.

What, then, is a spiritual song? It is the expression, or the natural outburst, of a heart that has been moved. There are many examples of such songs in the Bible. Take, for instance, the song of Hannah after the birth of her child (1 Samuel 2:1-10). How natural that is! How often people have tended to do that! Indeed, Mary, the mother of our Lord, did the same thing—we call her song 'the Magnificat'—and Zechariah, the father of John the

Baptist, burst into song after his son was born. Zechariah's song is a spiritual song, the expression of a heart filled with praise, thanksgiving and rejoicing. When people are filled with the Spirit, that is what one expects.

And, of course, we are told in Revelation, the last book in the Bible, that there is a great deal of singing in heaven. Listen to Revelation 5:9: 'And they sung a new song, saying, Thou art worthy'—they are talking about the Lamb of God, the Lion of the tribe of Judah, the victorious, glorified Christ—'to take the book, and to open the seals thereof: for thou wast slain, and hast redeemed us to God by thy blood out of every kindred, and tongue, and people, and nation.' Here is the massed choir of the redeemed bursting forth into song as they contemplate their glorious Redeemer and all he has done for them.

And in Revelation 14:3 we read: 'And they sung as it were a new song before the throne, and before the four beasts, and the elders'. It is a new song. There are always new songs in heaven. The theme is eternal and the singers are always seeing fresh aspects, so there is a new song, and then another, and another. That is the result of this inspiration, this being filled with the Spirit. 'And they sung as it were a new song before the throne, and before the four beasts, and the elders: and no man could learn that song but the hundred and forty and four thousand, which were redeemed from the earth.' The 144,000 is not to be taken literally; it is a symbolic number standing for completion: 12 x 12 = 144; then 1,000 = 10 x 10 x 10—it is perfection. *All* the redeemed are joining together to sing. That is how we will be singing in glory, and in Ephesians 5:19 the apostle is saying that even here we are making a start.

Joyful praise
Now there are those who teach, and I am inclined to agree with them, that Paul may very well have been saying something like

this: When you meet together, there is great joy within you because you are Christian people filled with the Spirit. How are you going to express this? Well, sing some of the old psalms of Israel, if you know them. In addition, some of you, under the influence and inspiration of the Spirit, may compose hymns, hymns of praise to God and to the Lord Jesus Christ. So bring them with you and sing them, and get other people to join with you in singing them.

As for songs, there is a suggestion here of something more spontaneous, of some extemporaneous utterance. As I have said, there are instances in the Scriptures of godly people suddenly having an awareness of what is happening, and of the truth, and bursting forth into song.

Nothing but psalms?

There, it seems to me, is a definition of the words used by the apostle. But we cannot quite leave it like that because, as I said, there have been good people in the church who have held the view that the apostle is saying here that you should sing nothing but psalms. There are some who would even go so far as to suggest that it is sinful to sing anything else. But that seems to me to be a very tragic position to be in. I feel that this view so militates against the spirit and context and atmosphere of this statement by Paul that I would like to turn aside and look at it with you for a moment.

There are certain good reasons, it seems to me, for asserting that it is erroneous to say that the praise of the church should be confined to the singing or chanting of the psalms. Here are some of them.

A Gentile church

Ephesians was, after all, written to a Gentile church, and the strong likelihood is that the vast majority of Paul's readers would not have known the book of Psalms in detail. The Jews would, and there were no doubt some Jewish members of the church. That is why I am leaving open the possibility that Paul may not be ruling out singing from the book of Psalms. It is possible that the Jews sang the psalms, but this is very different from saying that all Christians had to sing nothing but the psalms. Moreover, as we have said, we must remember that people did not have books as we now have them. So the Gentiles could not have sung the psalms out of a book.

Early writings

One of the first historians in the Christian church, a man called Eusebius, wrote: 'Beside the psalms, other compositions were sung in the early church.' That is a very important statement.

Furthermore, we know from the writings of Tertullian—a great man in the early church, who was born around AD 150 and went on living till about AD 220 or 230—that Christians used to meet together for what they called 'a love feast'. There are references to these meals in the Scriptures, and those who are familiar with the history of the evangelical awakening of two hundred years ago will know that the whole idea of the love feast was revived by the early Methodists, who would meet together to partake of the Lord's Supper and to remember his death, but also to rejoice and praise God together.

Now Tertullian tells us that in the love feast this happened: 'After water for the hands, and lights have been brought in, each is invited to sing to God in the presence of the others from what he knows of the Holy Scriptures, or *from his own heart*.' Now *that* is the important point, 'from his own heart', and that, I feel, is what we are dealing with in Ephesians 5:19— this extemporaneous composition that had been composed at home as a hymn, or this song into which the worshipper burst forth under the inspiration of the Spirit at the moment.

There is also evidence from non-Christian sources. For instance, in a letter to the Emperor Trajan, who was emperor of Rome from AD 98 to 117, the younger Pliny, governor of Bithynia, wrote that the Christians of Bithynia met on a fixed day before dawn and recited an antiphonal hymn to Christ as a god. That letter is a fact of history, and establishes the point that in the early church other compositions were sung, in addition to the book of Psalms and portions of Scripture.

Songs addressed to the Lord Jesus Christ

Then my third reason is that after writing, 'speaking to yourselves in psalms and hymns and spiritual songs', the apostle goes on to define his words. He adds, 'singing and making melody in your heart to the Lord'. Everybody is agreed that this is a reference to the Lord Jesus Christ, so Paul's words clearly indicate that new songs were written to him and in his praise.

'Every one of you hath a psalm'

Then, as my fourth reason, let me take you to 1 Corinthians 14:26: 'How is it then, brethren? when ye come together, every one of you hath a psalm, hath a doctrine, hath a tongue, hath a revelation, hath an interpretation. Let all things be done unto edifying.' Now this is a fuller description of what used to happen in the early church when Christian people met together.

Again, the whole context is that of people speaking under the inspiration of the Spirit. The apostle had to write because there were excesses in the church at Corinth. There was a certain amount of disorder. Two or three would be speaking in tongues at the same time; two or three would be prophesying; two or three would be singing. There was an element of ecstasy, and Paul wrote that if a stranger came into the gathering and heard that sort of thing going on, he would come to the conclusion that they were all mad. So Paul gives instructions on how to bring about order and control.

Now you notice the things the apostle puts together. He says that one person has a psalm, another a doctrine, another a tongue, another a revelation, another an interpretation.

But what does he mean there by 'psalm'? He may mean that some members of the church were familiar with the book of Psalms, and were therefore able to sing a psalm. But it seems to me—and not only to me (Charles Hodge, for instance, and others take the same view)—that the context indicates that Paul is almost certainly not referring to a psalm from the book of Psalms but to a psalm that has been composed under the inspiration of the Spirit. The doctrine, tongue, revelation and interpretation have all been given by the Spirit either at the time or immediately before. So it seems rather remote to assume that Paul is just saying here that while one of them speaks in tongues, and others suddenly have an aspect of truth revealed to them, there is one who does nothing but recite one of the psalms out of the Old Testament. Such an interpretation of 'psalm' takes it out of its context.

'I will sing with the spirit'

Then notice Paul's words in 1 Corinthians 14:15: 'What is it then? I will sing with the spirit, and I will sing with the understanding also.' When the apostle sang 'with the spirit', what was he singing, do you think?

These words refer to a state of ecstasy in which, under the inspiration and impulse and movement and guidance of the Spirit, Paul was giving utterance to things that he had never before contemplated. As people spoke in tongues, so they sang in the spirit. Paul is not talking about singing the psalms of the Old Testament. You do not do that 'with the spirit'; you do that 'with the understanding'. But here is a spiritual, ecstatic singing, and that is the context of the entire fourteenth chapter of 1 Corinthians.

Early church worship

But let me say something that is perhaps more relevant to our immediate position. All this is of great significance because I am hoping, God willing, to suggest to you in our next study that the church—speaking generally—is as she is at the present time because she has departed so far from the kind of situation that Paul is describing here.

Let me, therefore, put it like this. We see here a typical meeting of the early church, with men and women filled with the Spirit. The apostle is not giving an account of what should happen in a formal service such as we normally have today, or such as you may have in a cathedral. We are in an entirely different realm. I see very little in common between what the apostle describes here and the church services with which we are familiar. Let us remember that the contrast in Paul's mind is with that old type of jollification when people were under the influence of drink. The kind of meeting that Paul is describing has something of that element in it. There is joy, there is freedom, there is happiness, there is inspiration, and we must not shut that out.

A 'happy evening'

I myself have no difficulty in understanding this because of a type of meeting that was once very popular in Wales. It was called a 'happy evening' or a 'happy night'. What happened was that a number of friends and neighbours would meet together in a farmhouse. There would be an enormous kitchen, with the fire on the floor looking up into a great chimney, and people would be coming together to have a happy time. They would start by talking, and then someone would tell a story he had heard. There was always a man who had a harp, and after a while they would say to him, 'Why don't you sing to us?' And he would sing. He might have composed a little poem especially for the occasion, and he would sing it, accompanying himself on the harp. Or perhaps he

19

would come without preparing and they would say, 'Well, think of something now.'

I am not, of course, describing a Christian occasion; it was a secular gathering. The people would be drinking and the singer, in his semi-drunken condition, would improvise. Then another man would recite a poem that he had composed, or he would compose a poem at that moment and recite it, and there would be great cheering and clapping. Everybody would make some sort of a contribution. That was the great characteristic of these evenings. Nobody was silent, just looking on; everybody took part. There they were, all of them, having a happy evening together in this free atmosphere, worked up partly by the drink, perhaps, and partly by the excitement of it all.

It was the same in the ancient pagan world. Indeed, most nations have had and still do have something or other corresponding to the Welsh 'happy evening'. There are people, I gather, who meet together in public houses and other places to have what they call a 'sing-song'. It is the same idea, only there is less spontaneity and fewer individual contributions.

Now we must bear in mind those kinds of gatherings as we try to understand Paul's words in verse 19. Paul is writing of men and women who are filled with the Spirit of God, and each one has something: a psalm, a doctrine, a revelation, an interpretation, a tongue. Here they are, over-full, as it were, and wanting to give utterance. And as each one gives his contribution, the others rejoice and praise God together. They are all in a state of great joy and glory and happiness.

In times of revival

I think that the accounts of some of the great revivals in the church give us the best understanding of what Paul is talking about here. The only difference is that in a revival there is an out-pouring of the Spirit. Over and above their being filled with the

Spirit, the people experience an element of ecstasy. So you will read that in a meeting during a revival there are sometimes a number of people doing different things at the same time. Three or four may be praying together, another singing, another groaning in agony, crying out for salvation. It seems to be pandemonium and disorder, but it is not; it is a kind of 'divine disorder', as someone once put it. That is the extraordinary thing about a revival: you seem to get disorder, and yet there is an order running through it all; everybody is edified and everybody is filled with the spirit of rejoicing.

In the same way here, in the church in Ephesus, one person under the inspiration of the Spirit and seeing some aspect of truth suddenly bursts into a song. Or another, having had some revelation of God at home and having written a hymn of praise to the Lord Jesus Christ, has brought it to the meeting and speaks it or sings it. The others are astounded and moved and say, 'Let's learn this', and they all begin to sing it together.

Clearly, from Paul's words here in Ephesians 5:19, and especially in 1 Corinthians 14, there was always a liability, not to say even a tendency, to disorder in these meetings, because the people were all so anxious to express what they felt and had experienced and knew. To the Corinthians Paul says in effect, 'You must sing or speak one at a time, and if you see that someone else has something to say while you are on your feet, then sit down and let that person speak.' Read 1 Corinthians 14 again.

Needed advice
But the interesting point is that the early Christians were so filled with the Spirit that Paul had to write as he did. He would not have written that to us, would he? He would not write it of a cathedral service. No, no; we tend to judge the New Testament meetings by those that we, in our deadness, are familiar with. But if you think that this is an instruction to people to have a drab,

21

solemn, dull service, where nothing is sung but psalms, then you have misunderstood the apostle's words.

It is the very opposite of that. Here is joy, here is inspiration, here is revelation, here is something that is given by the power of the Spirit. And the apostle says: Now you must control this. 'Let all things be done decently and in order' (1 Corinthians 14:40).

The inspiration of the Spirit

I would add a sixth point to the argument I have just given in reply to the view that it is sinful to sing hymns. To say that nothing is worthy of being sung in God's praise save the biblical psalms leads to this position. If it is wrong to sing an extra-biblical hymn or psalm composed in praise of God, then extempore prayer is wrong, and any praise and worship and adoration and thanksgiving that someone may give under the inspiration of the Spirit in prayer is wrong. But that is a monstrous suggestion. It cannot be wrong. It is inspired by the Spirit

We must be careful that we do not limit the Holy Spirit, and that we do not become guilty of quenching the Spirit in a legalistic manner. The Holy Spirit not only enabled the biblical authors to write this inspired, authoritative, inerrant Word of God, but, thank God, the same Spirit can enable a little preacher to preach; the same Spirit can enable a writer to compose a hymn; the same Spirit can enable an artist to paint a picture in representation of the glory of God. Have you not read the story of Handel composing his famous *Messiah*—that extraordinary masterpiece composed in a few weeks? What was the explanation? Handel gave it himself when he said, 'I did feel as if all heaven were open before me.' That was the inspiration of the Spirit; there is no question about it. Our hymns are not Scripture, but that does not mean that they are not inspired. Of course they can be! And so many of these hymns are obviously gloriously inspired by the Spirit of God, whose concern is to glorify the Lord Jesus Christ.

'Decently and in order'

Now I understand my good friends who sing nothing but psalms and who say, 'Look at some of the hymns that are sung. Look at the doggerel. Look at the words that are almost blasphemous.' I agree with them a hundred per cent; I try never to give out such hymns or such choruses. But their error is entirely because they do not realise that the opposite of what is bad is not nothing; it is what is good! There were excesses in the church at Corinth, but what does Paul say? Does he say, 'Never speak in tongues again, never prophesy again, never give vent to these feelings that you have within you'? He says nothing of the sort! He says, 'Carry on, but do everything decently and in order.' The opposite of excess is not silence but control. That is a ruling that is of universal application.

The history of revivals

And I end with this. The history of the church shows us clearly that whenever there is a genuine revival, whenever the Spirit of God really does come down and fill the church, then there are many new hymns. Martin Luther composed hymns when he first saw the truth and was filled with the Spirit. Then look at the eighteenth century. Look at men like Charles Wesley, John Cennick, Philip Doddridge, William Williams in Wales—all these mighty composers of our glorious hymns. These hymns were born in revival. Of course, when people are filled with the Spirit, they want to praise God and to praise the Lord Jesus Christ. Revivals always lead to hymns and spiritual songs.

But I can even say this: sometimes the order is reversed and hymns *lead* to revival. I am thinking of one notable instance. In 1763, after a period of drought and spiritual dearth in the church in Wales, William Williams wrote the hymn translated 'O'er the gloomy hills of darkness'. At that time he published a volume of his hymns and spiritual songs, and the people began to sing them,

23

and it led immediately and directly to another outpouring of the Spirit of God.

'Quench not the Spirit'

So let us ever remember that the antithesis of disorder is control. Let us be careful lest in our dislike of doggerel and poor hymns and sloppy, sentimental singing, we do not become guilty of quenching the Spirit and putting a limit upon what the Holy Spirit can do with Christian people who have been filled with the Spirit.

The whole atmosphere in the church at Ephesus was charged with the Spirit, and found expression in psalms and hymns and spiritual songs. So let us avoid all excesses and let everything be done decently and in order. But above all, let us 'quench not the Spirit' (1 Thessalonians 5:19), but rather be filled with him and give evidence of that.

2
Melody in the heart

*'Speaking to yourselves in psalms and hymns
and spiritual songs, singing and making melody
in your heart to the Lord.'*
(Ephesians 5:19)

We are continuing with our consideration of the apostle's words in Ephesians 5:19. In this verse Paul is looking at how Christian people express the joy of salvation that they have in the Holy Spirit when they meet together as companies and communities. We have seen that Paul contrasts the drunken orgies indulged in by pagans and unbelievers with the convivial, happy meeting together of Christian people, and indicates the ways in which Christians should express the joy they feel within themselves.

But now we come to the second part of this verse, to the statement, 'singing and making melody in your heart to the Lord'. I do not believe that this is an additional exhortation. It is not that Paul *was* talking about speaking and has now come to singing, but that here he is giving an indication, or an explanation, of the way in which we should sing these psalms and hymns and spiritual songs. This is both necessary and important, as I think we shall see, because in any expression of praise we must concentrate attention not only upon the words but also upon the tune, or the way in which the words are expressed.

Our whole emphasis in our last study was on the fact that we should be very careful not to quench the Spirit, that in our fear of excesses we should not go to the other extreme and put a limit upon the free, spontaneous, inspired expression of the Christian soul and spirit under the leadership and guidance of the Holy Spirit. But having done that, we must now follow the apostle as he puts an emphasis upon the complementary truth.

There are certain truths that must always go together, and we are now going to look at the second half of one particular combination. On the one hand we have, 'Quench not the Spirit' (1 Thessalonians 5:19): on the other, 'Let all things be done decently and in order' (1 Corinthians 14:40), and in a fitting and worthy manner.

Yes, we must sing psalms and hymns and spiritual songs, and no limit must be put upon the freedom of the Spirit in that sense. But, as is always the glorious characteristic of the work of the Spirit— and as Paul makes clear in Ephesians 5:18—along with the stimulus, at one and the same time the Spirit also provides control. Wine does not do that; nothing else does. It is the unique mark of the leadership of the Spirit: the stimulus, the life, the power, but always the control and the discipline.

So it is to this aspect of the Spirit's work that we shall now turn. And we see at once what a wise teacher this great apostle was. How well he knew all of us, and how well he knew the danger of our always going from one extreme right over to the other! What a tragedy it is that we cannot keep the perfect balance that the New Testament observes! In our fear of one danger, we over-correct and go too far on the other side.

'Making melody'

Let us look first at Paul's terms. The original meaning of the Greek word 'making melody' is 'to strike the lyre' or 'to strike up a tune'. But it does not stop at that. By now, and indeed throughout the centuries, even in the time of the apostle, this term 'melody' has had a wider connotation.

Here are some definitions given in the *Oxford English Dictionary*: 'sweet music'; 'a beautiful arrangement of musical sounds'; 'beauty of musical sounds'; 'tunefulness'; 'the air'. It is important that we should realise all this, because I am arguing that in verse 19 the apostle is giving us a definition of what is, and what should invariably be, the characteristic of Christian music. And as he is dealing with the whole question of how we should conduct ourselves when we meet together to worship and to praise God, it is most important that we should be clear about the meaning of his words.

Paul says, 'making melody in your heart to the Lord', and this is always the characteristic of Christian music. There is such a thing as Christian music, as there is Christian poetry and Christian art. I have a feeling that one of the great troubles in the church today is that we have forgotten the definitions of these words and have foolishly tended to go in for 'art for art's sake'. 'Melody', says the apostle. So what does he mean? Let me tell you first of all what Paul does *not* mean.

Not 'cleverness'

The apostle is saying that when Christians express their praise and sing their psalms and hymns and spiritual songs, they should not try to be 'clever'. Cleverness is never the characteristic of Christian music, nor, indeed, of anything Christian. The Christian is never to be merely clever. If any preacher of the gospel, myself included, gives an impression of cleverness in his preaching, then it is bad preaching. It is totally unlike the New Testament and totally unlike that which is inspired by the Holy Spirit. Cleverness belongs essentially to the world.

Do you see why I am saying all this? You are aware of the modern vogue, not only in music but also in art and poetry. The idea today is that you must not be melodious; you must be clever. Melody is out of fashion. What is really admired today is a sort

27

of series and collection of clashing discords—not, as we read in our definition, 'a beautiful arrangement of musical sounds' but, apparently, a deliberate attempt to make the music *not* beautiful. But then it is clever! People today despise anything tuneful and melodious, just as they dislike the poetry that people used to like. They are not interested in rhyme, rhythm and balance. Poetry must be jerky, staccato. So if you read the music critics in the papers you will find that it is the clever, clashing, cacophonous music that is popular. The beautiful element seems to be at a serious discount. And I am concerned to emphasise that this is not Christian.

Beauty and harmony

We must not be devotees of this modern craze for ugliness. What is Christian is always beautiful, it is always melodious, it always leads to peace, to harmony, to rest and to joy. And that is because it is produced by the Holy Spirit. 'Be filled', says Paul, 'with the Holy Spirit..' Among those other people, with their bacchanalian songs and so on, you can expect all sorts of noises and clashes and discords. But Paul's whole point is that Christian music is exactly opposite to that. It always has melody, this form and beauty, as its most essential characteristic. And this is true of Christian art in its every expression.

Now I am arguing that it is very important that the Christian church should realise this. She must stand in opposition to the ugliness that is so evident in the worldly conception of every kind of art today. Christian music is not merely an opportunity for people to show their cleverness in execution and their inventiveness, going out of their way, as it were, to avoid melody, never putting in the note you would expect, but deliberately inserting a wrong note so as to keep the music always in some state of flux without any beauty of form. Merely to be clever is the mark of the world, with its barren intellectualism and its hardness and its coldness. This is so evident in the modern world that it is our duty to go out of our way to counteract it and to show the beauty, the harmony, the peace and the joy that belong to Christian praise.

Not superficial and flippant

I started with cleverness because it is so obvious in the world today, but it is not the only characteristic to be avoided. True melody is never merely light or flippant, or what is called 'jiggy' and syncopated. The world likes light and flippant music. But that is never Christian. Whatever is Christian cannot be trite— that is impossible. Whatever is Christian is always essentially simple, but simplicity is not incompatible with depth; indeed, they generally go together. So the apostle is telling us here that as we sing these psalms and hymns and spiritual songs we must not let ourselves be carried along by something superficial—that is worldliness.

No term is so abused today as this word 'melody'. Sometimes on the radio, when you are waiting for something better, you hear people crooning and droning—and speaking of 'melody', of all words! What a foul perversion of a beautiful and glorious term! Melody is never trite, never flippant, never showy, never theatrical. That is incompatible with melody, as it is incompatible with Christianity.

The people in Ephesus had become Christians, but they were not yet perfect, and they tended to do certain things in the old manner. Paul's whole emphasis is that they must put a stop to that and do everything in the Christian way. And melody is the essence of that way.

Worthily

Let me sum it up like this: the apostle is saying that as we thus sing praise to God, we must do it in a manner that is 'worthy of' or 'suited to' who he is. As Paul writes to the Philippians: 'Only let your conversation be *as it becometh* the gospel of Christ' (Philippians 1:27). That is it! Our praise to God must be becoming, it must fit in, it must be all of one piece and of one pattern. The form must correspond to the God we are addressing. You cannot have great and glorious words and a jiggy tune.

If you are filled with the Spirit, and are allowing the Spirit to lead and guide you, then there will be no trouble about this, because he who gives the words will also give the music. He will give you the air, the tune, everything you need, and everything will be perfectly matched.

'In your heart'

Let us continue with our definition of Paul's terms. Now the phrase 'in your heart' is not merely something thrown in, it is not just here by accident, so what does Paul mean? Again, let us first be clear about what he does *not* mean.

Not privately, heartily or sentimentally

The apostle does not mean that in the innermost part of your being, in your heart, you should privately, secretly, make melody and sing praises to God. Some people have interpreted these words in that way, but the whole context is against that meaning. Paul is not concerned here to tell Christians what they should do when they are alone: he is emphasising what they should do as they gather together. Let me remind you that he is making a contrast between the times when non-Christians meet to drink wine and have their sing-songs in what they think are happy and jolly get-togethers, and the times when Christians meet together in community.

It is equally important that we should realise that Paul does not mean 'heartily'. Many have become confused and have thought that he is saying, 'Let us sing together our psalms and

hymns and spiritual songs, singing and making melody heartily.'
You are familiar with that exhortation, we hear it so often these
days! But the apostle says, 'in your heart', not 'heartily'. Heartily
means something very different, as I shall show you.

There are people who seem to think that Christian praise
should be sentimental. We are familiar with such words and
tunes, but that is not Christianity, that is not what is meant by 'in
your heart'.

No, by this phrase the apostle means that you must be controlled by the Holy Spirit in the very centre of your being. The
word 'heart' here, as so often, indeed generally, in the Bible,
refers not only to the seat of the emotions, but to the whole person. As Christians we must realise what we are doing; we must
be well aware of what we are singing.

Now those people in their drunken meetings are not interested
in anything. They do not think at all; indeed, they cannot think.
They just shout and sing. That is their idea of making themselves
happy, and the more they sing and the more they shout, the more
intoxicated they become, and the worse and worse it gets. But the
Christian is the exact opposite: he sings and makes melody in his
heart—and that includes the understanding.

Engaging the mind . . .

As Christians led by the Spirit, says Paul, you realise that you are
in the presence of God and that you are singing praises to God.
You know that you are there to glorify and magnify God's great
and holy name. Our Lord himself put this quite plainly to the
woman of Samaria: 'Ye worship ye know not what . . . God is a
Spirit: and they that worship him must worship him in spirit and
in truth' (John 4:22, 24). Worship is not a matter of place. It is not
'this mountain', says our Lord, nor is it 'Jerusalem'. And it is not
about forms and ceremonies. It is a matter of the Spirit. And that
is precisely what the apostle is saying here.

31

You are filled with the Spirit and the Spirit enlightens your heart. And that includes your mind, your understanding, your reason. You are not merely singing, Paul says, you are meditating. You realise what you are doing; you are careful and thoughtful. It is a very intelligent type of singing.

The psalmist puts emphasis upon the same point in Psalm 47: 'Sing praises to God, sing praises: sing praises unto our King, sing praises. For God is the King of all the earth: sing ye praises with understanding' (verses 6-7). The understanding is always involved in every action of the Christian. This, to me, is a very wonderful statement that we are looking at. It brings out that Christians always know what they are doing. They must never be thoughtless; they must never be unintelligent. The element of reason, understanding and thought is an essential part of whatever they do, because they are men and women who have been enlightened. They are no longer fools, but are wise, aware of what they are doing.

And Christians are not to be guided by non-Christians. It does not matter how great a musician a man may be, if he is not a Christian, I do not listen to him. I am not interested in the opinions of musicians who are not Christians, because they cannot give an opinion on Christian praise, which is something particular, governed by the Christian understanding that is given to us as the result of being filled with the Spirit.

. . . and the emotions

But, of course, Christian praise is not confined to the intellect. Paul's words indicate that the Christian sings to God with feeling. It is not to be done mechanically. It is not to be a dull repetition. No, says the apostle, if you are filled with the Spirit there will be love and joy within you, and you will be anxious to manifest this. So you will be singing with the whole of your being. 'Bless the LORD, O my soul: and all that is within me, bless his holy name' (Psalm 103:1). Not the mind only, but also not the feelings only, because your praise then becomes maudlin senti-mentality. The glory of the Christian position is that because the mind and the emotions are engaged, there is true melody. You are singing praise unto the Lord in a worthy and fitting manner.

There, it seems to me, is the essential definition of the apostle's words. Now it is important to emphasise that we need to *think* about this whole question of Christian praise. We are exhorted to consider it. We take part in it, so we must understand it.

Practical implications

So let us now try to apply these definitions. What do they mean in practice? What do they warn us to be careful about?

Words first

The first deduction I would make is that we must ever remember that we are not to concentrate only on singing the tune. The moment we do that, we have already departed from the apostle's instruction. The words come first—they are more important than the tune. Of course, the words and the tune should come together, married and blended together in order to give expression to our praise. But there is nothing quite so fatal as to be singing the tune only, without paying any attention to the words.

Let me illustrate what I mean. There is nothing that so appals me as to hear what happens when Christians sing that great hymn 'Jesu, lover of my soul' to the tune 'Aberystwyth'. When they come to the second half of the third verse, which goes like this—

> *Just and holy is thy name,*
> *I am all unrighteousness;*
> *Vile and full of sin I am,*
> *Thou art full of truth and grace.*
> Charles Wesley

—almost invariably they shout the whole of that statement, 'I am

33

all unrighteousness', and especially, 'Vile and full of sin I am'.
They shout it as if they are glorying in it, and emphasise it more
than they do the last line, 'Thou art full of truth and grace'. And
why do they do that? It is because they are carried away by the
tune, and are not paying attention to the words. They are not
thinking about what they are singing. Here is a tune that goes
well, so everyone is carried away by it.

Let me give you another illustration. There is a well-known
chorus beginning, 'God is still on the throne'. Do you recall the
tune to which it is generally sung? I would not hesitate to assert
that it is blasphemous! The tune is light and jiggy. It trips along.
Blithely we sing, '*God* is still on the throne.' No, no; we are carried
away by the tune, and are not paying any attention to the words.

Singing divorced from the Word

I want to put a further problem to you for your consideration, a
problem about which I am becoming increasingly concerned. Is
it ever right, do you think, to divorce the singing of hymns, or
any expression of Christian praise and worship, from the preaching of the Word?

As Protestants, we have always insisted that the sacraments
should never be separated from the Word. This is a battle we
have fought over against the Roman Catholics, the Anglo-
Catholics, and all other catholics. It is always characteristic of
Catholicism that the sacraments are divorced from the Word, so
you can take the sacrament in a service where the Word is not
preached. Now Protestantism has always—and rightly, in the
light of the Scriptures—protested against that. But I am now ask-
ing whether you do not agree that the same rule should apply to
the singing of hymns, carols or any music that is designed to
express Christian praise and worship.

I was brought up in a tradition in which we had what were
called 'singing festivals', when we spent a whole day singing

familiar hymns and learning new ones. But I wonder whether that is really justifiable in the light of the apostle's teaching. Is it not inevitably the case that the tunes become more important than the words? I know the reply goes, 'But we open the service with a reading of Scripture and a prayer, and a word is given now and again.' But is that enough? Should you have a service that consists almost entirely of singing? I am of the opinion that the apostle Paul would say no to that.

I do not care what you are singing, whether carols or anything else; the singing must never be the main part of the meeting—it is a part, but never the whole. The singing must never have this prominence, it must never be divorced from the Word—or, at the very least, if you are going to separate the two, the meaning of the words must be made plain and clear. The man responsible for the meeting should read the words and comment upon them, urging upon the people a realisation of what they are going to sing.

The end of all this is something we are all familiar with, if only from the newspapers. Every year, in the Football Association Cup Final, it is now the tradition for that great concourse of people to sing, 'Abide with me'. Are they interested in the words? No, they like the tune. There are people singing, 'Abide with me, fast falls the eventide . . . Hold thou thy cross . . .', who do not believe in the cross. They are not interested in it, and are not even thinking about it as they sing the words. That is the extreme, of course, and it is outside the church, but I would suggest that inside the church we are often guilty of the same excess, the same error.

Let me put this to you in some words that were written by the great St Augustine. Augustine felt that there was strength and inspiration in hymn-singing, and he said this:

I perceive that our minds are more devoutly and earnestly elevated into a flame of piety by the holy words themselves when

they are sung, than when they are not, and that all affections
of our spirit by our own diversity have their appropriate
measures in the voice and singing, wherewith, by I know not
what relationship, they are stimulated.

Augustine is saying that he has discovered that singing does help
to kindle the flame of piety and of devotion within us; that when
the words are sung, they are more likely to have that effect upon
us than when they are merely spoken or recited.

But I must complete the quotation. St Augustine writes that he
fears 'the subtle beguilement of sweet sounds', and wishes at
times that they could be banished both from his ears and from the
church. He puts it like this:

When it happens to me to be more moved by the singing than
by what is sung, I confess myself to have sinned criminally,
and then I would rather not have heard the singing.

I think that is perfect! You see the balance? St Augustine says
that yes, singing is a great aid, it is a great stimulus, it helps to
bring out the spirit of devotion and of worship and of praise.
There is a great advantage in it. But he adds that we must always
be careful of a subtle danger—the danger of being more
impressed by the tune than by the words, the danger of being
carried away by the tune and forgetting the words. He is afraid
of the 'beguilement' of a beautiful tune. And he goes so far as to
say that when he has been so beguiled, he feels he has 'sinned
criminally'. Something has come in that is not a part of the leading of the Spirit.

And there is no question at all but that St Augustine is giving
perfect expression to the teaching of the apostle that we are considering together. There has to be a balance—the mind, the
words, the understanding, as well as the tune.

Emotionalism

Here in this verse we also see that there must not be a forced excitement of the nerves or of the emotions. Quite the opposite. That is why I emphasised earlier that Paul does not mean that we are to sing heartily. When he tells us to sing and make melody in our hearts to the Lord, he is incidentally saying: Do not sing too much. He is quite deliberately saying: Above everything, do not try to work up the meeting by forty minutes or so of preliminary singing.

Now singing before the service starts is the modern idea, is it not? 'Ah,' it is said, 'we must work up the meeting; we must get the people into a good mood, into a receptive frame of mind.' In other words, there are people who deliberately manipulate the nerves and make a direct attack upon the emotions, trying by means of the singing to stir up the congregation.

'Drunk' on singing

But there must not be too much singing, because you can become drunk on singing: you can go on singing and singing until, really, you are in such an emotional state that your mind is no longer operating. I have often seen that happen. Are the apostle's words compatible with the modern popular 'song-leader', who jumps into a pulpit or on to a rostrum and cracks a few jokes just to put people into a good mood?

I remember once going to a religious meeting that was held in a large tent. A man came forward at the very beginning to conduct the singing, and he made his jokes and laughed. Then I remember how he said—and it produced great laughter—'Now, let it rip!' Then, 'I didn't mean the tent, of course!' They laughed and laughed at that, but it is a complete denial of what Christian people should do. That is what happens in the drunken orgy: the jokes and the laughter and the joviality, so called. Such a jocular statement should not make us laugh. Rather, it is to be wept at.

Paul is talking about something diametrically opposed to a meeting led by a song-leader. He is talking about the leadership of the Holy Spirit, and the Spirit 'making melody in your heart to the Lord'.

There are some people who believe in working up a meeting by means of clapping. 'Why do you denounce that?' asks someone. 'Doesn't the forty-seventh psalm, which you have already quoted, start by making this very statement: "O clap your hands, all ye people; shout unto God with the voice of triumph"?'

Well, it seems to me that the answer is this: If you are so filled with the Spirit, and so moved by him, that you find yourself involuntarily clapping your hands, all is well. But that is very different from clapping your hands in order to work yourself and everybody else up into a state of excitement. When you are exhorted mechanically to clap your hands and stamp your feet and beat on some tambourine or other instrument in order to induce a sense of excitement, you are again being told to do exactly the opposite of what the apostle is saying.

In the same way, we must be careful about the musical instruments we use. There are musical instruments that are sensuous, that belong to the world. Saxophones and instruments of that type have no place in Christian worship; their sound is primitive, lacking the thoughtfulness and wisdom that characterise Christian music.

The wrong way round

To sum up this section, the apostle is not saying that we should sing until we make ourselves feel happy. He is saying, Look here! Because you are filled with the Spirit, and because he has shed this joy abroad in your hearts, you *are* happy. So give expression to your happiness by singing psalms and hymns and spiritual songs, 'making melody in your heart to the Lord'. But we have reversed all this. We say, 'These people have come to the meeting. They're jaded and tired, so we've got to work them up and get them into a good mood.' And so we sing and sing and sing, with all the accompaniments and all the modern trappings, until everyone is in a good mood.

'Let all the people sing'

So I come to my third deduction, which is an emphasis. You notice that the apostle addresses these words to *all*, rather than to some, Christians. Here you are, he says, you have gathered together, you Christian people. So now speak to one another in psalms and hymns and spiritual songs; join together in singing and making melody in your hearts.

This is Christian praise, and it involves all of us. So Paul cannot be talking of the congregation sitting and listening to the beautiful singing of a choir. That is almost directly opposed to what he is saying. Yet that is what we have come to. It is worse when the singing is by a paid choir, and still worse when the members of the paid choir, or the special quartet, are not even Christians but are brought in because they have good voices. Sometimes, both in this country and, even more frequently, in other countries, they arrive at the service just in time to sing, and then leave immediately afterwards!

But that is not what the apostle is saying. Here we have God's people all meeting together, filled with the Spirit, and they all take part because they are all sharers of the same Spirit and partakers in him. With our great, dignified cathedral services, where only the choir sings and nobody else ventures or dares to join in, we have departed far from the New Testament pattern. How can we forget the New Testament to such an extent?

We are all in this, my friends, and if you do not sing, there is something the matter with you. Why do you not sing? Do you not want to? Do you not want to praise God? *All* of you must mingle your voices, you must all sing together, says the apostle. It is because of excesses that people have gone to the extreme of having choirs only. But that is not the answer—to go to the opposite extreme is never the answer to a problem.

The right way

There is a right way for a congregation to sing. What is that? Well, sing together, says Paul, 'making melody'. This is where the harmony, the balance and the control come in. In congregational singing you do not behave as if you were a soloist. A soloist is meant to sing alone, but the ideal and glory of congregational singing is that there is balance and wholeness, they are all one, there are no voices standing out above the others. The prominence of particular voices destroys the element of harmony that is meant to accompany a beautiful melody. And to display your individual voice when a congregation is singing is to deny the apostle's instruction.

But that happens, does it not? It is a great temptation when you have a good voice. You can show it by starting the line before everybody else, or by holding out at the end when everybody else has finished, so that your voice is heard in all its beauty and glory. Yes, but that destroys the whole spirit of what the apostle is saying. He says: You must sing together, not to show off your voice, not to display yourself and thereby cause irritation to everybody else who is round and about you. If you have a great and powerful voice, then moderate it when you are with others, otherwise you will be disturbing the harmony. You are always to be guided by the Spirit.

What is the result of the Spirit's leading? Paul tells us in Galatians 6:22-23: 'love, joy, peace'—peacefulness. Nothing that jars or irritates anybody else, no self-display, no standing out. You become merged in the body and praise God together. 'Longsuffering, gentleness, goodness, faith, meekness'—which is the opposite of showing your voice and being proud of it. And finally, 'temperance', which means self-control. 'But', someone says, 'I have such a great and powerful voice.' Then control it! 'I have wonderful breath control and I can go on.' Well, do not if others do not. We are all one here.

Is it not wonderful that the apostle should have written all this? Do you realise how tremendously important it is? Are you sensitive to these things? I confess that I am. Very often when I stand in this pulpit I can hear people who are failing to obey the apostle's teaching in this respect, and they are a hindrance to my preaching, and to my spirit. Are you aware of these departings from the presiding glory of the Holy Spirit, and from the meekness, the temperance and the peace, and all these other glorious qualities that he always produces?

Worship that glorifies God

Everything we do in these gatherings in God's house is important. We meet together to praise God and to worship and adore him. What a terrible thing if we should go away having merely given rein to our emotions and the animal part of our beings! What if we should only have displayed ourselves, our cleverness, our ability, our voice? That is a denial of Paul's teaching. Do not be like those drunken people: they keep on interrupting one another, each wanting to show that he is better than everybody else, each displaying himself, boasting of himself.

You are not like that, says the apostle. You are not filled with wine, which leads to excess, you are filled with the Spirit. Therefore your meetings are characterised by peace, by melody, by harmony, by meekness and self-control; they show this balance, this concern about the whole body, this concern for the glory of God. 'Singing and making melody in your heart to the Lord; giving thanks always for all things unto God and the Father in the name of our Lord Jesus Christ.'

Well there it is! This is the kind of sermon that a man would never have decided to preach, or have chosen to preach. But if you have learned nothing else from this, I trust that you have learned the wisdom of working systematically through a book of the Bible, not picking out texts here and there. Have you ever heard a sermon on this before? Probably not. These are the things that we ignore, and so, in practice, the Christian church often denies her own belief, departing from the New Testament pattern to such an extent that you really can scarcely recognise her as being the same church.

So, to sum it all up: Do not quench the Spirit in your fear of the excesses of hymn-singing and so on; but, on the other hand, be careful to ensure that everything in the realm, or the freedom, of the Spirit is done decently, in order, with temperance and with self-control. 'For God hath not given us the spirit of fear; but of power, and of love, and of a sound mind [of discipline]' (2 Timothy 1:7).

May God enable us, therefore, in all we do, whatever our gift, be it of song or of speech, of poetry or of art, to bear these truths in mind, and to be Christian. Let the element of beauty, of harmony, of peace, of melody, this glorious perfection of the Spirit—let that be manifest in all that we do, that it may ever be to the praise of the glory of his grace.

3
The song that never ends

*'Speaking to yourselves in psalms and hymns and
spiritual songs, singing and making melody
in your heart to the Lord.'*
(Ephesians 5:19)

Everything that we have been saying about verse 19 is of
great importance. The apostle has all along been emphasising and contrasting the essential difference between what the
world and what the members of the Christian church regard as
happiness and joy and conviviality. In every step, in every detail,
we have noticed the difference. Everything we do as Christians
is diametrically opposed to the way of the world. In place of
ribald ballads we have psalms and hymns and spiritual songs.
And we do not even sing in the same way.

But the supreme, the final, difference between non-Christians
meeting together seeking happiness, and a group of Christian
people expressing their happiness, is to be found in the *theme* of
their songs. And so the apostle leads up to it—'singing and making melody in your heart *to the Lord*'.

What do people who are not Christians sing about? Well, if you
analyse their songs, you will find that in various ways the singers
sing about themselves and about one another. Had you ever
realised, I wonder, that the world is always singing about itself—
itself in terms of individual people, and itself as represented in
nations—national songs, full of boasting and pride? And then the
people toast one another, and praise one another, and go on

43

singing about one another. That is the characteristic of worldly jollification and worldly attempts to be happy. We all know, of course, that if we praise others, they will probably praise us! So the people of the world spend their time in a kind of mutual admiration society. This is not only true of their songs, it is also true of their literature. The world is always revolving round itself.

But when, in verse 19, we look at Christians singing together, we notice immediately that not only is the form different, but that the very substance, the theme about which they are singing, is entirely different. For Christians it is always the Lord—'singing and making melody in your heart to the Lord'.

The Lord Jesus Christ

It is generally agreed that the words 'the Lord' refer to the Lord Jesus Christ, as the apostle makes clear in the next verse, where he says, 'Giving thanks always for all things unto God and the Father in the name of our Lord Jesus Christ.' It is important to remember that in the New Testament the term 'the Lord' generally stands for God the Son rather than God the Father. And in explaining the words 'psalms and hymns and spiritual songs' we showed that these are specifically addressed to the Saviour, the Son, the second person in the blessed Holy Trinity.

But we have a further proof that the words 'the Lord' refer to the Lord Jesus, a proof that puts this question beyond any dispute whatsoever. When he was talking about the coming of the Spirit, our Lord said, 'He shall not speak of himself . . . he shall glorify me' (John 16:13-14). The Holy Spirit was sent to do that. The Son glorified the Father, the Spirit glorifies the Son, and through him, of course, the Father also. That is the special, the particular, work of the Spirit. And since the apostle says in verse 18, 'Be not drunk with wine, wherein is excess; but be filled with the Spirit',

44

it is an inevitable deduction that it is the Son whom the Spirit-filled worshippers are praising and adoring.

The test of the Spirit's work

It is always very important for us to remember that the way to test whether or not we are experiencing the work of the Holy Spirit upon us is just this: does it lead us to worship and praise the Son and to desire to sing to his glory? Most of the aberrations that have troubled the church from century to century with regard to the doctrine of the Spirit have arisen from the failure to apply that test.

People tend to judge the operation of the Spirit by experiences, by powers, visions, ecstasies, thrills, healings and things like that, things that savour of the miraculous. But the New Testament is very careful to tell us that those are very dangerous and misleading tests. Because we can be so easily deceived, we are told to 'try the spirits' (1 John 4:1)—to prove them and examine them. And, in the last analysis, praise of the Son is the test. It does not matter what marvellous things you may be enabled to do, if your experience does not lead you to glorify the name of the Son more than ever before, you have very good presumptive evidence for saying that whatever it comes from, it is not from the Holy Spirit.

The Holy Spirit does not draw attention to himself. He does not draw attention to us. He does not draw attention primarily to particular results. He glorifies the Son. He, as it were, hides himself, even as the Son did when he was here in the world. Our Lord came incognito, in the likeness of a man. And in a measure that is true of the Spirit. He seems to hide himself in order that everybody may look at the Son. Therefore, if you hear people talking perpetually about the Spirit and hardly ever about the Son, you have good reason for believing that they may well be the subjects of a delusion.

45

Yes, says the apostle, when people are filled with the Spirit, they speak to one another in psalms and hymns and spiritual songs. They sing and make melody in their hearts to the Lord— always to the Lord!

On a more ordinary level, we also see here a very good test as to whether or not we are Christian at all. Let there be no mistake about this. It is of supreme importance for us all, and it can never be stated too frequently. It is our attitude, our relationship, to the Lord Jesus Christ that determines whether or not we are Christians. Muslims worship God. The Jews worship God. But the special, the differentiating thing about Christians is that Jesus Christ is always essential and central; without him there is nothing. He is the beginning and the end, the Alpha and Omega. There is no Christianity apart from him, and indeed, and still more serious, he is the only way to God. Our Lord says, 'No man cometh unto the Father, but by me' (John 14:6).

The Christian is someone who delights in the Lord, who delights in telling forth his praise. Now I want to hold you to this because, I repeat, it is a very good way of testing ourselves. Yes, it is very interesting to look into the exact meaning of psalms and hymns and spiritual songs, and it is important to offer God worship worthy of him, and to understand how that is to be done. But God forbid that we should stop there, at what I would call the mechanics, the means. It is all meant to bring us face to face with him.

The focus of praise

So Paul tells us that we must sing and make melody in our hearts *to the Lord*, and by these words Paul means in particular that we are to focus on the Lord himself, not on what he has done for us. We always want to go to what he has done for us, to what he has given us. But first we must consider him as he is in and of himself. We must not start even indirectly with ourselves. The

subject of what he has done for us is raised in the next verse—
and it is all true—but before you come to that, says the apostle,
praise him for himself, praise him for who he is. Look at him.
Forget yourselves for the moment; forget even the benefits of the
Christian life, and just look at him, consider him, and praise his
name.

The testimony of the Scriptures

This is, of course, the great theme of the Bible itself from
beginning to end. Every remote reference to him is a song in
some shape or form. In Isaiah chapter 40 we read these great
words of poetry: 'Comfort ye, comfort ye my people, saith your
God.' Why? Well, because he is going to come: 'Behold your
God!' An Old Testament prophet cannot consider the possibility of his coming, he cannot see it dimly afar off, without being
thrilled to the very marrow of his being. Inspired by the Spirit,
he cannot write in a prosaic manner about the coming of the
Son of God. No, no; he says, 'lift up thy voice with strength'—
shout; 'make straight in the desert a highway . . . Every valley
shall be exalted, and every mountain and hill shall be made
low' (verses 1, 9, 3-4). Why? Because your God is coming and
all flesh shall see him.

Every anticipation of the coming of the Son of God into this
world always moved these Old Testament prophets to their very
depths and made them produce the most glorious masterpieces of
poetry and prose. Again, let us remember that they were not simply setting out to write great literature. We must always get rid of
that notion. This is the work of the Holy Spirit. He inspired the
language, the very words, and so they sang like that.

Go back further, and you will find that even a hireling prophet
like Balaam could not help praising him. When Balaam is given
his vision, he talks about the coming of the Lord and is lifted up
above himself and above the ordinary (Numbers 23–24). You

47

find the same note of praise in that last great statement of Moses, and in the final words of Jacob; it is everywhere.

And, of course, when our Lord actually did come and was born, the first thing that happened was that the angels began to sing. You remember the music that was heard by the shepherds watching their flocks by night. The angels were singing and celebrating his birth. The New Testament starts with singing and making melody. The angels make melody in their hearts as they think of him and as they sing his praises together. They sing his glory, we are told, in heaven. Everything connected with him always leads to an outburst of praise and of singing and thanksgiving from those who are nearest to him, those who see him, those who know him as he is.

Consider him!

And all this becomes important for us because, as I have been reminding you, it is such a thorough test of our whole profession of the Christian faith. Look at these hymns of ours; look at the joy felt by the hymn-writers at the very mention of his name:

> *How sweet the name of Jesus sounds*
> *In a believer's ear:*
> *It soothes his sorrows, heals his wounds,*
> *And drives away his fear.*

John Newton

Does it? It should! It always has done when people have really known him. Yes, says Paul, this is the characteristic of people who are filled with the Spirit. They sing and make melody in their hearts to the Lord. When you come together, that is what you will be doing. Our Lord himself said, 'For where two or three are gathered together in my name, there am I in the midst of them' (Matthew 18:20). And as Christian people realise his presence, they pour out their hearts in melody in the detailed way that we have been considering.

This, then, is the question that comes to us: Do we do that? Do we feel a desire to do that? What is Christianity to us? Sometimes I think that some of us give the impression that it is a terrible task and a most awful burden to be a Christian, and that it makes us more miserable than all other people in the world. 'Ah,' you say, 'I'm sad because I see the sin, because I understand it all.' Yes, but that is only one side of your experience as a Christian. There is this other side—the Lord! Is this subjectivity not our most fatal trouble? We spend so much time looking at ourselves, taking our own spiritual pulse, wondering what is happening to us, and desiring this and that benefit, that the result is that we do not contemplate him. We do not consider him. We do not know him. There is no joy and no happiness in our experience. But what the apostle commands the Ephesians to do is to rejoice and make melody in their hearts.

The Spirit, as he fills us, will always lead us to praise the Lord Jesus. So we must be careful to obey his promptings. And the most common prompting of all is the prompting to read the Bible, because it is here that we see him and can meet with him. Of course, we can meet the Lord without the Word; sometimes he meets us when we are not reading it, but we meet him most frequently there. He has given it in order that we might see him. Here is the portrait, here are the pictures. And the inevitable effect of seeing him will be that we will sing and make melody in our hearts to him.

His person

What will we sing about? Our song will be of the glory of his person, of the majesty of the Lord. 'In the beginning was the Word, and the Word was with God, and the Word was God' (John 1:1). Oh, we must meditate about these things: his eternity; his everlasting glory with the Father; not created, only-begotten, co-equal, co-eternal with his Father in every respect. That is the person about whom we are to sing. And we must concentrate upon this. We must remind ourselves of it. If we read the Bible, of course, we will be reminded, provided we do not read it mechanically.

Do not misunderstand me. I am a believer in systematic Bible reading, but there can be a terrible danger even in connection with that. 'Ah,' you say, 'what's my portion for today? I must read that.' And often your chief concern is simply to read the daily portion. But you must stop and think about what you are reading; you must meditate; you must give time to it. You are going to meet him there, so give time for him. Do not rush past it in order that you may go and do something else. We must stop with these things and think about them and meditate on them.

His glory

The Bible tells us about this everywhere. The author of the letter to the Hebrews says: 'God, who at sundry times and in divers manners spake in time past unto the fathers by the prophets, hath in these last days spoken unto us by his Son . . . who being the brightness of his glory, and the express image of his person . . .' (Hebrews 1:1-3). He is God, the effulgence of the glory of the everlasting God, God the Son, the second person in the blessed Holy Trinity.

Then notice what the writer also says: 'by whom also he made the worlds'. John says the same thing: 'All things were made by him; and without him was not any thing made that was made' (John 1:3). Look at creation: the mountains and the valleys and the rivers and the streams and the flowers and the animals and human beings. Where has it all come from? This blessed Lord has made it all. He is the one who made all things—with the Father and the Spirit, of course, but it is particularly his work.

I cannot stay with these specific themes. I am simply trying to indicate to you what the Holy Spirit does when we allow him to lead us, which is what is meant by being filled with the Spirit. It means that we are subject to him, that he is guiding and directing us in all things. He will always lead us to Christ, and this is one way in which he does that.

The glory and majesty of the Son is a theme that is sufficient to occupy us for all eternity. 'Father,' he says at the end of his life, 'glorify thou me with thine own self with the glory which I had with thee before the world was' (John 17:5). And there is another request of his in that high-priestly prayer: it is a prayer that we may behold his glory (John 17:24). That is his supreme desire for us. We belong to him, and he wants us really to know him, to see him as he is, to know something about this transcendent, indescribable glory—'that they may see my glory'. Do we contemplate the Son in this way and think of his majesty and his glory and his everlasting greatness?

His incarnation

Then think of another theme—the wonder of our Lord's incarnation. The apostle Paul could never come anywhere near this without bursting forth into some sort of singing, into some kind of hymn of praise. He makes a magnificent statement of it in his first letter to Timothy, a verse we have already looked at: 'And without controversy great is the mystery of godliness: God was manifest in the flesh, justified in the Spirit, seen of angels, preached unto the Gentiles, believed on in the world, received up into glory' (1 Timothy 3:16). What a theme! That is just a synopsis of the incarnation, but there it is. The apostle liked to look at it, the whole movement, the marvel and wonder of it. And the great apostle finds himself moved to the very depths of his being. Listen to his powerful statement in Philippians 2:5-11:

51

Let this mind be in you, which was also in Christ Jesus: who, being in the form of God, thought it not robbery to be equal with God: but made himself of no reputation, and took upon him the form of a servant, and was made in the likeness of men: and being found in fashion as a man, he humbled himself, and became obedient unto death, even the death of the cross. Wherefore God also hath highly exalted him, and given him a name which is above every name: that at the name of Jesus every knee should bow, of things in heaven, and things in earth, and things under the earth; and that every tongue should confess that Jesus Christ is Lord, to the glory of God the Father.

The trouble with the Christian church is that she spends all her time in talking about the Christian attitude towards this, that, and the other—war and bombs and social conditions. That is all right, I agree that those subjects have to be included, but they most certainly do not come in at the centre, and should not be the message that is preached every Sunday. Here is the centre!

It is because the church does not know her Lord, and fails to marvel at and be moved by the incarnation, that she counts so little in the world. She has no vigour, no life, no power. She is talking about *things*, when she ought to be talking primarily about *him*. It is because the world does not know him that it does not listen to his teaching about particular matters. And it will never listen until it knows him, and understands the reason why he came into the world.

An incomparable theme
There he was in the form of God. Of course, he was God, God the Son. That was the form in which he had existed from all eternity. Do you want something to sing about? Do you say that you are unmoved, and that you do not feel a great well of song with-

in your heart, that there is no melody in your life? Well, if you want something to give you that melody, here it is. Look at this!

He was from eternity in the form of God, but he did not regard that as a prize to be clutched at all costs; instead, he 'made himself of no reputation, and took upon him the form of a servant, and was made in the likeness of men'. What is the matter with us, Christian people, that our hearts are not fired as we think of the incarnation? He left the courts of heaven; he came down to live on earth as a man; he was born as a baby in Bethlehem. Listen to Charles Wesley stating this:

> *Mild, he lays his glory by,*
> *Born that man no more may die.*

He is still God in all the fullness of his being. He cannot lay the Godhead on one side, he cannot empty himself of that, but 'Mild, he lays his glory by'—he puts aside the sign of it, the external appearance. He comes in the form of a man, not in the form of God, though he is God.

> *Christ, by highest heaven adored,*
> *Christ, the everlasting Lord;*
> *Late in time behold him come,*

—after so many thousands of years—

> *Offspring of a virgin's womb.*
> *Veiled in flesh the Godhead see!*
> *Hail the incarnate Deity!*
> *Pleased as man with men to dwell,*
> *Jesus, our Immanuel.*

Immanuel—God with us.

That is magnificent poetry, is it not? Yes, but it was not Charles Wesley: it was the Spirit in him inditing it, inspiring it.

Of course, here was a man filled with the Spirit who knew his Scriptures, and he saw it and put into verse all that Paul is describing in his great song in Philippians chapter 2.

I must also quote two verses of a great hymn by Isaac Watts, which expresses it perfectly:

> *The spacious earth and spreading flood*
> *Proclaim the wise and powerful God;*
> *And thy rich glories from afar*
> *Sparkle in every rolling star.*
>
> *But in his looks a glory stands,*
> *The noblest labour of thy hands;*
> *The radiant lustre of his eyes*
> *Outshines the wonders of the skies.*

Have you seen it? Have you had a glimpse of it—'The radiant lustre of his eyes'? We are told in the book of Revelation that his eyes are 'as a flame of fire' (Revelation 1:14). Yes, but there is a lustre there, a glory, and, while on earth, a mildness and a meekness. Of course he is incomparable! He stands alone. Is that theme not enough to occupy not only your time in this world, but your eternity as well?

His life on earth

But go on to consider the life our Lord lived on earth; his obedience to Joseph and Mary; his humility. Here is one who made everything, and yet look at him, the lowly, the humble, the meek Jesus. Look at his sympathy, his compassion. Look at him, ready to stop at any moment to deal with a case of need and suffering. Look at his understanding, even of the tax-collectors and the sinners. The religious leaders reviled him because of that and said that he was 'a man gluttonous and a winebibber, a friend of publicans and sinners' (Matthew 11:19). Oh, the wonder of his life on earth! Why don't we sing? Why isn't there a melody in our hearts as we contemplate this?

His offices

But then consider his perfection in his offices. 'Great *Prophet* of my God,' bursts out Isaac Watts. And that is what he is. Look at his authority. He begins to preach and to speak, and the people are amazed: 'For he taught them as one having authority, and not as the scribes' (Matthew 7:29); 'Never man spake like this man', said the temple officers (John 7:46). All right—put a tune to that, sing that. Look at him, praise him, his authority, his teaching.

Listen to his teaching about God. Here is one who knows God. He does not speak at second hand. He is not groping after God. He is not like the philosophers who have preached so much, written so much, and to whom the world listens so much. They are but speculating. But he has come from the Father. 'And no man hath ascended up to heaven, but he that came down from heaven, even the Son of man which is in heaven' (John 3:13). He knows: 'We speak that we do know' (John 3:11). Of course! He teaches about God with a finality seen in no other person.

Then listen to him in his teaching about us and about our salvation, and as he teaches about the course of history and the future of the world—'Great Prophet of my God'. There has never been anybody like this. Here is the teacher. He stands alone, and does not belong to any category.

Priest

But hurry on: consider the Lord Jesus as the priest. Look at him honouring the law of God. He was 'made of a woman, made under the law' (Galatians 4:4). Yes, and he kept it. He honoured it. He never broke a single detail, not a jot or tittle. In no respect did he fail. What was he doing? He was working out a righteousness for his people.

Then think of his suffering. Think of the contradiction of sinners that he endured while he was here. Look at his enemies. Look at the persecution. Look at the hatred, the malice, the spite, the spleen manifested against him, the spitting and the scorn. Does it not make you sing? This is the Lord of glory, the brightness of the Father's person, the express image of his person. And this is what is happening to him; he humbled himself to this. Does this not move us?

Go to Gethsemane and look at him, and you will feel like saying,

> *When my love to God grows weak,*
> *When for deeper faith I seek,*
> *Then in thought I go to thee,*
> *Garden of Gethsemane.*
> John Reynell Wreford

How often do you go there? Are you unhappy? Are you full of problems and difficulties and grumbles and complaints? In the name of God, I say to you, go to Gethsemane and look at him, your Saviour, your Lord, suffering there, sweating drops of blood for you.

Then look at him crucified upon a cross, suffering indescribable agonies, crying out his cry of dereliction—'My God, my God, why hast thou forsaken me?' (Mark 15:34). Dying! Who is dying? The one through whom all things were made. The Lord of glory dying, expiring, dead upon the cross. They take down his body and lay it in a tomb. What is he doing? This is his work as a priest. He himself is the offering.

And watch him as he goes on with his work as a priest. He passes through the heavens. He enters into the holiest of all—to offer to God what? Not the blood of bulls or of goats or the ashes of an heifer, but his own blood! What a theme! Every moment of it, every step of it, should move us to the depths and make us sing.

And then think of him there in heaven as the great High Priest doing his work of intercession. 'If any man sin, we have an advocate with the Father, Jesus Christ the righteous' (1 John 2:1). 'He ever liveth to make intercession for them' (Hebrews 7:25). He is the great Prophet and he is our great High Priest.

King

But thank God he is also the King! Here are the things that make people sing and rouse the melody in their hearts. The King! How do you know he is the King? I have described him crucified, dead, and buried. They rolled the stone in front of the tomb, and they sealed it, and the soldiers guarded it. But he burst asunder the bands of death. Death could not hold him. Why? Because he is the King. He is the Creator. He has all might and authority and power.

Then behold him ascending. Take a visit now to the top of Mount Olivet and see him rising to the skies. Who is this? This is the Son of God: 'Declared to be the Son of God with power, according to the spirit of holiness, by the resurrection from the dead' (Romans 1:4). Watch him as he rises and disappears. Where has he gone? He has gone into the heavens in order that he may sit down: '[He] sat down on the right hand of the Majesty on high' (Hebrews 1:3). And that is where he is now.

Lift up your hearts and think of him, you weary saints, you tired people, you men and women who are so subjective. Think of him, your Saviour and your God, seated at the right hand of God. 'All power is given unto me', he says, 'in heaven and in earth' (Matthew 28:18). Men are attacking you and reviling you, are they? They are making life difficult for you and making you unhappy. All right, think of him, your Saviour, as he is seated at the right hand of God. He is simply waiting until his enemies shall be made his footstool. For the day is coming when he will return to this world, fully visible, fully revealed in all his glory, no longer taking the form of a man, no longer as the babe, but as the King of kings, the Lord of lords, riding the clouds of heaven, surrounded by his holy angels. He will come to judge the world in righteousness and he will come to reign.

That is something of the theme of our song.

The mighty anthem

'Speaking to yourselves in psalms and hymns and spiritual songs, singing and making melody in your heart to the Lord', says the apostle. 'But how can I make melody in my heart?' asks somebody. 'I don't feel like singing.' My dear friend, consider him until you do! Ask the Spirit so to reveal him until you cannot keep silent. This is what you must do, says the apostle: 'Be filled with the Spirit.' And as you are led by him, you will look at the Son and you will not be able to contain yourself. You will burst forth into praise:

> *Let those refuse to sing*
> *That never knew our God:*
> *But children of the heavenly King*
> *May speak their joys abroad.*
> Isaac Watts

Do you sing, or do you say, 'Why didn't you deal with the present international situation? The world's in a terrible state. Why have you spent time telling us all these things we already knew?' I will tell you why: it is because you do not sing about them! And I sometimes wonder whether I should not go on just repeating this Sunday by Sunday until we are all singing and making melody in our hearts to the Lord. There is no greater insult to the person of Christ than to forget him because you are so interested in the state of the world, and so on. It comes near to being the final blasphemy.

Let us not be among those who, in their ignorance, refuse to sing. Rather, we want to say, do we not,

> *Brightness of the Father's glory,*
> *Shall thy praise unuttered lie?*
> *Break, my tongue, such guilty silence,*
> *Sing the Lord who came to die!*
>
> Robert Robinson

An endless theme

Robert Robinson was right. But we can only start on this theme. We can but say with Isaac Watts: 'Begin, my tongue, some heavenly theme.' You will not finish the song.

For once in my life I am sorry for people who do not understand Welsh! There is a Welsh hymn that puts perfectly what I am anxious to say at the moment. It says that far away in eternity the hosts of heaven will only just be beginning to sing his praise: '*Dechrau canu, dechrau canmol . . .*' (beginning to sing, beginning to praise). After the millennia have passed, and passed again, we shall only just be starting! We shall be only at the beginning of singing his praise. It is an endless theme. And what we are doing is but a continuation of what has been started in the past.

> *Their joy*

[the joy of those who have gone before us]

> *unto their Lord we bring,*
> *Their song to us descendeth;*
> *The Spirit who in them did sing,*
> *To us his music lendeth.*

His song in them, in us, is one,
We raise it high, we send it on—

What is it?

The song that never endeth.
Thomas Hornblower Gill

What a theme! No, we cannot get beyond beginning it, and we realise how poor we are and how feeble our words. So we go again to Isaac Watts, and we agree with him in singing:

Join all the glorious names
Of wisdom, love and power,
That ever mortals knew,
That angels ever bore;
All are too mean to speak his worth,
Too mean to set my Saviour forth.

A rehearsal

But let us begin this heavenly theme. Let us do our utmost. Let us allow the Spirit to move us and to inspire us. In this world we are simply in a kind of singing rehearsal. We are all just being prepared for the mighty festival of music and of song that takes place in heaven.

And they sung a new song, saying, Thou art worthy to take the book, and to open the seals thereof: for thou wast slain, and hast redeemed us to God by thy blood out of every kindred, and tongue, and people, and nation; and hast made us unto our God kings and priests: and we shall reign on the earth.

(Revelation 5:9-10)

That is what they are singing. And we shall join in the song. And then just as we think we have exhausted it, this is what will happen—we will say:

60

I beheld, and I heard the voice of many angels round about the throne and the beasts and the elders: and the number of them was ten thousand times ten thousand, and thousands of thousands; saying with a loud voice, Worthy is the Lamb that was slain to receive power, and riches, and wisdom, and strength, and honour, and glory, and blessing. And every creature which is in heaven, and on the earth, and under the earth, and such as are in the sea, and all that are in them, heard I saying, Blessing, and honour, and glory, and power, be unto him that sitteth upon the throne, and unto the Lamb for ever and ever.

(Revelation 5:11-13)

Do you not think that it is time you began to prepare for that? Do you not think that it is about time you began to tune your voice, to tune your heart, to get ready? Heaven will be a terrible place for you if you do not want to sing his praise, if you do not feel the desire, and if you do not know about him. Meet together, says Paul. Be filled with the Spirit, and sing and make melody in your hearts to the Lord, because you will hear the mighty anthem there, and you will be left alone and will not know what to do with yourself.

Oh, be ready for it! I know that the redeemed prepare for this because, after this mighty singing, I read that 'the four beasts said, Amen [So be it]. And the four and twenty elders fell down and worshipped him that liveth for ever and ever' (verse 14). That is how they sing about him in heaven.

The feeblest 'Amen'

We have seen how the saints sing about him and have sung about him on earth, so I ask you this one question: Have you heard something of the music? You may not be gifted, you may not be a great singer, but I ask this minimum of you: Do you want to say 'Amen'? Did you in your heart say 'Amen' as I tried so inadequately to hold the Lord Jesus Christ before you and to describe him to you?

As I have told you how people who see him thus sing about him, is there just a very feeble 'Amen' in your heart? If there is, thank God you are all right, you belong to him. The feeblest 'Amen' to all this is a sign that you are born anew, that you have received life from God. So encourage it! Go to the Scriptures. Be led, be filled with the Spirit, and then as you see him you will praise him without ceasing, beginning within your heart this song that never ends.

4
A life of praise

'Giving thanks always for all things unto God
and the Father in the name of our Lord Jesus Christ.'
(Ephesians 5:20)

It is clear that in verse 20 the apostle still has in mind the contrast between the Christian and the non-Christian. He empha-
sises this contrast in the earlier parts of this epistle in an attempt
to show the Ephesian Christians how, now that they are born
again and have received new life in Christ, their outlook will be
changed and their whole life will be essentially different from
before. Now he is coming down to the details, and we have been
looking at how all this shows itself in their relationships with one
another and in their common acts of worship and of praise to
God. So we come to Paul's words in verse 20.

'Giving thanks'

Perhaps nothing is more characteristic of people who are filled
with the Spirit than thanksgiving. They have a sense of gratitude
to God and are filled with praise for all his abundant and abound-
ing mercies.

Those who are not Christians do not thank God. If ever they
mention his name, it is to complain, criticise and grumble. They
never talk about God, they never believe in worshipping or
thanking him for anything. But then a war suddenly comes, and
they say, 'Is this your God? Why does God allow war?' Such

people always have their catch questions: 'If there is a God, and if he is a God of love, as you say, then why this spastic child?' And so on. No thanks at all. No praise.

In contrast, Paul writes of Christians 'giving thanks always for all things unto God and the Father in the name of our Lord Jesus Christ'. This is the inevitable result of the work of the Holy Spirit. Certain things invariably happen when the Holy Spirit is present in power. You cannot read the account of any revival without finding that it has always been an occasion of great thanksgiving and praise. The great hymns that come out of revival are always hymns of praise. In times of revival, people are conscious, above all, of the goodness and the grace and the mercy of God, and they pour forth their hearts in thanksgiving.

The work of the Holy Spirit

In the very first chapter of this epistle, Paul reminds the Christians in Ephesus that ever since he was with them he has been praying for them. He says:

> [I] cease not to give thanks for you, making mention of you in my prayers; that the God of our Lord Jesus Christ, the Father of glory, may give unto you the spirit of wisdom and revelation in the knowledge of him: the eyes of your understanding being enlightened

—that is always the work of the Spirit. And what does he do? Well, he opens our understanding—

> that ye may know what is the hope of his calling, and what the riches of the glory of his inheritance in the saints, and what is the exceeding greatness of his power to us-ward who believe.
>
> (Ephesians 1:16-19)

So when the Holy Spirit is present in power, when people are filled with the Spirit, their minds are enlightened; they are given knowledge and understanding; they are aware of certain things about God and his relationship to them. And, of course, you cannot have that knowledge without being moved by it.

But the Holy Spirit also moves and works upon the heart. His operations are never confined to the mind alone. He starts by enlightening the mind, but the difference between those who merely have intellectual knowledge of the truth and those who are really filled with the Spirit is that the hearts of the latter are moved. The Holy Spirit has a mighty influence upon the hearts of men and women. He softens them, warms them, melts them and stimulates them. Christians whose minds are enlightened and whose hearts are moved by the Holy Spirit are inevitably filled with an overflowing spirit of thanksgiving and praise to God, and though they feel all this, they would still like to thank God more and more.

> *Come, thou Fount of every blessing,*
> *Tune my heart to sing thy grace.*
> Robert Robinson

A test

Now this raises a question for us—a question that is a very good test of the nature and character of our Christian life and of our spiritual tone. To what extent is there this element of praise and thanksgiving in our life and experience? Stop for a moment and ask yourself this: When I am on my knees in the presence of God, what do I do there? Analyse your prayers. To what extent do you thank God always for all things? How much time and attention do you give to praise and thanksgiving? How much to petition?

I wonder how we emerge from this examination. It is the relative proportion of petition and praise in our prayers that tells most exactly the measure, the degree, of the Holy Spirit within us. People whose spiritual lives are weak and spasmodic spend their time in petitioning God, and there is no praise at all. It is a curious fact that here are people who want this and that, and feel they do not have what they want, and then doubt whether God is dealing with them fairly. But, of course, there is only one explanation: these people are not aware of the truth concerning God. They are probably not obeying him. They are not conforming to the life and to the pattern of our Lord, and that is why they are not being blessed more than they are. But those, on the other hand, whose minds are enlightened and whose hearts are moved, want above everything else to praise and thank God.

Formality

One of the most alarming and appalling features of the way in which, alas, most of us live, is our failure to thank God. We are all guilty. When we do thank God, we pray mechanically. In a sense, I do not know of anything that is more terrible than formal thanksgiving. Now I am not saying that we should not even give thanks formally; it is quite right that we should, but it is a terrible thing if it is merely formal. You know what it is like when people give you formal thanks for something—it does not help you or give you any pleasure at all. You are much more aware of the formality than of the thanks.

We either pray formal prayers or we have a series of petitions for ourselves and for various other people in whom we are interested. And what makes it still more terrible is that we are rather proud of ourselves for having done that—especially if we have a prayer list and offer up petitions for a number of people. Now do not misunderstand me: it is very good to pray for people. If you have promised to pray for a missionary or someone in need, do so! We can never do this too much. But I still say that the measure of our spiritual tone and whole condition is the element of thanksgiving and of praise that is in our prayer life and in all our thinking about God. 'Giving thanks always.'

What a happy people Christian people are! Here you are, Paul says. When you meet together, you are not like those people in their drunken orgies with their ribald songs and attempts at jollification. Yours is a true happiness, and it comes welling up out of your hearts. There is nothing formal. You make melody in your hearts and you thank God from the heart.

'To God and the Father'

Secondly, the apostle tells us to whom we are to give our thanks: 'Giving thanks always for all things unto God and the Father'. By that, of course, Paul means God the Father, but this is how he commonly says it, and I think he puts it in this way very deliberately.

God the Creator

When Paul says 'God', he is thinking of the almighty and eternal God, God as the Creator. He is the author of all being, and we should give thanks to him for that. He is the giver of every good and every perfect gift and he is the author of all life, of the whole universe and of everything that is. So, Paul says, give thanks to God.

And offering thanks is a permanent duty. It is something that everybody should be doing, even those who are not Christians. God is to be praised: 'Let the people praise thee,' says the psalmist (Psalm 67:3). All people! The whole universe should be thanking and praising God as the giver of all gifts, the source and the fount of every blessing.

God the Father

Yes, but the apostle at once hurries on to add 'and the Father'. And it is here that he has a special word for the Christian. To the Christian, God is not only God the Creator, the everlasting God; he is, in particular, the Father. He has become one whom

Christians can address as their Father. Now this is not true of everybody. The notion of the universal fatherhood of God is not taught in the Scriptures. God is the Creator, and you can say that he is Father in that sense, but he is not Father to all and sundry. He is only Father to those who are in Christ Jesus. John writes: 'He came unto his own, and his own received him not. But as many as received him, to them gave he power [authority] to become the sons of God' (John 1:11-12).

Our Lord said to the Jews who did not believe in him: 'Ye are of your father the devil' (John 8:44). Do not say that God is your Father. You say that you are children of Abraham, that you are children of God, but you are not. If you were, you would not be rejecting me and reviling me and blaspheming me. 'Ye are of your father the devil, and the lusts of your father ye will do.' No, God is not their Father. They are in the relationship of created beings to Creator, but no more.

But here, in his epistle to the Ephesians, the apostle reminds Christian people that they are in an entirely different category. God has become their Father, in and through our Lord and Saviour, Jesus Christ.

Paul is very careful to write 'and the Father', in order to remind us of what our duty is. He wants us to examine ourselves and know what we should be doing as people who are filled with the Spirit. In other words, the thanksgiving and praise of the Christian should be altogether greater and more abundant than that of anyone who is not a Christian.

So let us now look at how the apostle Paul divides up this teaching.

'Always . . . unto . . . God'

Paul says 'always', and he means this literally. We are always to give thanks to God as God. 'But how does that work out in practice?' asks someone. It means something like this.

Life

First, we should always be thanking God for the very gift of life itself, for it is God who has given us our being. 'It is he that hath made us, and not we ourselves', as the psalmist reminds us (Psalm 100:3). For all their cleverness, human beings cannot create life. God is the author of life. He gives us all existence. And this is something for which we should thank him. He has made us and put us into this world. It is a tremendous fact. We shall never understand it fully, but we should thank God for it.

But we do not stop at that. Consider other reasons for always thanking God. Think of some of the provisions he has made for us and for our lives in this world. It is only right that we should remind ourselves of these things from time to time.

Marriage and the family

It is God, let us never forget, who ordained marriage. It was God who gave man a helpmeet, the woman, to be with him. Marriage is not a human institution. It is not a good idea that some man suddenly thought up. It is not something that evolved as human beings developed. No! It was God who deliberately ordained it, planned it, fashioned it and told man and woman all about it.

And God at the very beginning ordained the family as the fundamental unit, so that when we come into this world we are not left, as it were, on the cold doorsteps of life, but enter into the bosom of a family, who surround us with love and care and protection. Do you ever thank God for that? We are not born like animals and allowed more or less to struggle and fend for ourselves from the very beginning. Not a day should pass but that we thank God for our families.

Physical needs

Then think of food, clothing and shelter. It is no use talking to me about tractors and modern implements and fertilisers. They would be of no value at all if God did not send the rain and give the sun. Our daily bread comes from God, in spite of our efforts. All our work would be useless but for God who is the giver. 'Giving thanks always'—day by day. We should never eat food without giving thanks to God, because it has come from him.

Likewise our clothing, shelter, health and strength are gifts from God. And this is universal. In the Sermon on the Mount, our Lord reminds us that God 'maketh his sun to rise on the evil and on the good, and sendeth rain on the just and on the unjust' (Matthew 5:45). So the evil and unjust, too, should be thanking God for the sunshine and for the rain. And if *they* should, how much more those of us who are Christian!

Skills and abilities

Then think also of the personal gifts that we all enjoy. Everybody is endued with certain powers and faculties and propensities. You may be clever in one respect or another—mathematically, scientifically, musically, dramatically. Think of all the gifts that people have: some have the gift of understanding; others are wonderful with their hands and can make and fashion things; others have discernment and judgement.

Yes, but now here is the question. From where did you get those gifts? Have you created them? You are proud of them, perhaps, but have you a right to be? Did you produce them? Have you generated them? Did you conjure them up? Are they really the result of your efforts? Of course not! You were born with them, and it is God who gave them to you. We glory in someone like Shakespeare, but we should thank God that he gives human beings such gifts. We are living in an age when we praise men and women as if they have done everything, but they could not have done anything without the ability that God gave them. That is scriptural teaching. 'What hast thou that thou didst not receive?' (1 Corinthians 4:7).

It is only as we begin to consider all that God in his love has given us that we not only praise him aright, but know how to live aright. Think of all the trouble that has arisen in the world and in the church because men and women are proud of their abilities. Other people envy them, while they in their turn despise those not so gifted. It is all due to the fact that none of them realises that they have all received their gifts from God. He is the giver of every good and every perfect gift. So we should be giving thanks to God always for all these things. Do we—or do we take them for granted?

God's patience

Then think of God's long-suffering, his kindness to us, his patience with us, with all of us. 'It is of the Lord's mercies that we are not consumed' (Lamentations 3:22). The world is in a terrible state, and the foolish people, the ignorant people, say, 'Where is your God? Why does God allow this?'

But what we should all be saying is this: 'How does God tolerate us at all? Why are things as good as they are?' It is nothing but the long-suffering, the compassion, the kindness of God. How can he stand it? Why does he not wipe us out of existence? Why does he not chastise us with an awful severity? That is how we ought to be speaking.

Yes, but then go on to the second part:

'. . . and the Father'

It is only the Christian who can always thank the Father. We thank him for all that he sends us through his Son. 'Thanks be unto God for his unspeakable gift' (2 Corinthians 9:15).

We say we are Christian people. Very well then, why is it that we do not spend all of our time in thanking God for the fact that he has ever looked upon us at all? We, like everybody else, were the children of wrath; we were born in sin—'In sin did my

71

mother conceive me', said David (Psalm 51:5). We are children of iniquity, every one of us. We all deserve hell and nothing else. Does anybody dispute that? Examine your life, then. Have you thanked God for all his goodness to you, for his very gift of life, that he has given you a soul? What do we deserve at the hands of God? We have broken his laws. 'All we like sheep have gone astray' (Isaiah 53:6). We have all followed our own devices. We deserve nothing but punishment and hell.

Forgiveness and new life

But God has looked upon us with a piteous and a merciful eye. He has chosen us and called us out of darkness into his most marvellous light. In spite of our sin and rebellion and recalcitrance, God has loved us with an everlasting love and has sent his only Son into our world, even to the death of the cross, in order to save us and redeem us. He has forgiven us freely. He says, 'I have blotted out, as a thick cloud, thy transgressions' (Isaiah 44:22). He has thrown our sins into the sea of his own forgetfulness. We stand before him justified, reconciled, absolved from all our sin. Is it surprising that the apostle says, 'Giving thanks . . . *always* . . . unto the Father'?

But wait a minute, we have not finished—God has given us new life. We are made partakers of the divine nature; he has put his Holy Spirit to dwell within us. He has delivered us from the thraldom and the tyranny and the sin of the world. He looks upon us as his children; the very hairs of our head are all numbered. He leads, he guides, he cares for us in his wonderful providence.

Present blessings and future hope

Then think of the blessings God gives us in connection with the life of the church: all we inherit by way of knowledge, exposition of the truth, by the lives of men and women who have gone before us. He has brought us into a large and wealthy place.

And then think of the prospect that lies ahead of us. The prospect of going to glory to be with Christ, to spend eternity in the presence of God, to be in the renovated, regenerated earth that is coming, the new heavens and the new earth where righteousness dwells, to reign with Christ as kings, to judge the world, to judge angels! All that is coming, and he is preparing us for that. It is because of things like this that the apostle says, 'Giving thanks always'.

Whatever you are feeling, whatever is happening to you, these facts, if you are a Christian, are always true. God saw you before the foundation of the world, and wrote your name in the Lamb's book of life. Before the foundation of the world! You!

'Ransomed, healed, restored, forgiven'

What is the matter with us, that we do not give thanks to God the Father, always? He has chosen us. He has separated us from the world. He has put us into Christ, made us members of the body of Christ. He has this marvellous plan and programme for us. He loves us with an everlasting love. This relationship of the Christian to God the Father is permanent, it is certain, it is always there, and always true. So why are we not always thanking him every day of our lives?

If we do not thank God, there is, of course, only one reason: we do not think about these things. We just say, 'I'm a Christian', and then put that into a compartment. I have sometimes put it like this: if we are not astounded every day of our lives that we are Christians, then we are very poor Christians. If we are not thrilled at the fact that we are heirs of eternity and of glory with Christ, if that does not daily thrill us to the marrow of our beings, then there is something wrong with us.

We get excited about all sorts of things, do we not—little successes, things that happen to us, or that we hope are going to happen, or that might happen—all the thrill of anticipation. Christian people! We say that we are Christians, that we are in Christ, that glory is awaiting us. But where is the thrill and the excitement? Where is the thanksgiving and the praise? The apostle is right, is he not? 'Giving thanks always'—always, always, without ceasing. There must never be any intermission.

We must stir ourselves up to realise these truths. We must ask God to fill us with his Spirit. We must avoid everything that grieves the Spirit, and then, being filled with the Spirit, we shall be aware of these things, constantly meditating upon them, and we shall sing:

> *Praise, my soul, the King of heaven,*
> *To his feet thy tribute bring;*
> *Ransomed, healed, restored, forgiven,*
> *Who like thee his praise should sing?*
> *Praise him! Praise him!*
> *Praise the everlasting King.*
>
> Henry Frances Lyte

'For all things'

But wait a moment! The apostle does not only say, 'Giving thanks always', but 'for all things'. Does this 'all' really mean all? Of course it does! It means everything. You cannot separate the 'all' and the 'always'. If you are always giving thanks, you must of necessity be giving thanks for all things, and the apostle means that: he means giving thanks in detail and deliberately.

'What?' asks someone. 'Am I to give thanks for trials? For troubles? For tribulations? For infirmities? Am I to give thanks to God when things go wrong?' The answer is, 'Yes!' Paul not only says it here, he says it elsewhere. He says it in Romans 8:28: 'We know'—we Christian people—'that all things work together for good'—now we must not put any limit on that because there is none—'to them that love God, to them who are the called according to his purpose.' All things! I do not care what they are, put them all in.

Listen to Paul again in 1 Thessalonians 5:18: 'In every thing give thanks: for this is the will of God in Christ Jesus concerning you.' Then in Hebrews 12:5-11, the writer tells us to give thanks for chastening, while James goes even further and says, 'My brethren, count it all joy when ye fall into divers temptations' (James 1:2). 'Temptations' there means 'trials', and trials, says James, should make you rejoice. The apostle Peter has exactly the same teaching. He says:

> Who are kept by the power of God through faith unto salvation ready to be revealed in the last time. Wherein ye greatly rejoice, though now for a season, if need be, ye are in heaviness through manifold temptations: that the trial of your faith, being much more precious than of gold that perisheth, though it be tried with fire, might be found unto praise and honour and glory at the appearing of Jesus Christ.
>
> (1 Peter 1:5-7)

A biblical example

But how do we give thanks to God in difficulties and trials? Well, let me take a notable New Testament illustration. In Acts 16, you will find an account of a visit paid by Paul and his companion Silas to the town of Philippi. All they were doing was preaching the gospel. And they worked a miracle there: they cast out an evil spirit from a girl possessed with the spirit of divination. And for that they were arrested and treated shamefully. They were scourged (that is, their backs were beaten with sticks and cords), and they were thrown into the innermost prison, where their feet were fastened in the stocks. You cannot imagine anything much worse than that, can you? And yet this is what we are told in verse 25: 'And at midnight Paul and Silas prayed, and sang praises unto God.'

I wonder what we would have been doing if we had been there. Paul and Silas could have grumbled and asked God what he was doing with them, why he was treating them like that. They were his good servants, so why had he allowed such treatment? Why was he so unkind and unfair to them? But instead, they prayed and sang praises to God. And, we are told, the other prisoners heard them. At midnight, they kept the other prisoners awake. Why? Because they were thanking God to such an extent, and singing so loudly, that the prisoners could not sleep! With their feet in the stocks in the innermost prison, Paul and Silas were 'giving thanks always and for all things unto God and the Father'!

But how can one do this? Well, Paul and Silas were filled with the Spirit and the Spirit led them. This is how it works, and this is what Paul and Silas probably did unconsciously.

If you find yourself in adversity, you do not sit down and say, 'Isn't it terrible? Isn't it awful? Why should this happen to me?' Instead, you say, 'All right! I'm in trouble, but I'm a Christian still. I know I've been chosen by God before the foundation of the world, and God so loved me that he sent his only Son into the world to die for me. He loved me and he gave himself for me. Though my feet are fast in the stocks, that is still true. So, thank God!'

And then there are all the other things, all that God has done for the Christian. Go through them: 'Count your blessings, name them one by one.' And you will begin to thank God because they remain true in spite of your adversity.

'for the name of Christ'

And there is another very wonderful and comforting thought that will make you thank God, though everything is going against you. This is how Peter puts it in his first epistle: 'If ye be reproached for the name of Christ, happy are ye' (1 Peter 4:14).

You may be suffering at this moment because you are a Christian. The people of the world do not like a true Christian, and they try to 'get it out of him', as they put it. But:

> If ye be reproached for the name of Christ, happy are ye; for the spirit of glory and of God resteth upon you: on their part he is evil spoken of, but on your part he is glorified. But let none of you suffer as a murderer, or as a thief, or as an evil-doer, or as a busybody in other men's matters. Yet if any man suffer as a Christian, let him not be ashamed [let him not be cast down, let him not be unhappy]; but let him glorify God on this behalf.

> (1 Peter 4:14-16)

So if things are going against you, if you find that you are suffering simply because you are a Christian, then, far from being cast down, 'glorify God on this behalf'. It is a wonderful privilege. They are treating you as they treated your Lord and Master before you, and the moment you begin to think like that, you praise God. You cannot stop it. You are thanking God for his goodness to you.

Necessary discipline

Then go on to consider this. When things have gone wrong or you find yourself in trouble, it is always good to ask questions. Do not grumble and complain. Instead, ask, 'I wonder whether I stood in need of this. Is this perhaps a bit of chastisement that I'm receiving from the hand of God?'

Now do not run away with the notion that I am saying that every illness or accident, or everything that goes wrong, is always chastisement—I have just been saying that it may be caused by the enemies of God. But sometimes it is, quite definitely—illness included. It is not always, but it can be. The psalmist tells us,

'Before I was afflicted I went astray' (Psalm 119:67). He was a good man, a godly man, but he had gone astray.

So say to yourself, 'I wonder whether I was beginning to get into a position in which I needed to be pulled up. Was I beginning to go astray? I wonder if this has happened to me because God was trying to keep me from sin. I wonder whether I was on a pathway that might have led me into terrible trouble if God in his goodness had not interposed. He has held me up. He has prevented me from going right to the end of where I might have landed.'

Then ask yourself, 'I wonder whether I've been tending to live a little bit independently of God. Things have been going well with me. I've been blessed. Nothing has been lacking. But have I been forgetting God? Have I been thanking him as I should? Have I been as regular in my duties to God as I should have been? Have I been praising him? I wonder whether this has happened in order to pull me up and make me examine myself and remind myself of all these things. Have I perhaps been tending to forget that, after all, I am but a pilgrim in this world, that I am a child of eternity, and that I always ought to be preparing myself for that which is coming to me as God's dear child?'

Ask yourself those questions, and you may well come to the conclusion that your difficulties are a bit of chastisement that God is giving you because he loves you. The writer of Hebrews says, 'Whom the Lord loveth he chasteneth, and scourgeth every son whom he receiveth' (Hebrews 12:6). If you are not receiving chastisement, he says, you are bastards! You ought to worry more if things never go wrong than if they sometimes do go wrong. Chastisement is a sign that we are children of God.

God's fatherly love

The consideration that God may be chastising you for your good, leads you to faith in his fatherly love. You say: God is my Father. I don't understand what's happening to me now, but I know this:

God moves in a mysterious way,
His wonders to perform . . .

Behind a frowning providence,
He hides a smiling face.
William Cowper

And the moment you arrive at all these conclusions, you begin to praise and thank him. You say:

His love in times past
Forbids me to think
He'll leave me at last
In trouble to sink.
John Newton

He cannot! To do so would be to deny his own eternal constancy. It would be to deny the fact that he is 'the Father of lights, with whom is no variableness, neither shadow of turning' (James 1:17).

And so, having reasoned it out, you come to the position that you not only do not complain, you are not only content with your lot, but you even rejoice in it. And you say:

Thy way, not mine, O Lord,
However hard it be.
Horatius Bonar

There is nothing like knowing that you are in the hand of God. And it is better to be in trouble, knowing you are in the hand of God, than to have everything going well without having this blessed assurance that you are in the centre of his will. Indeed, if you work out this argument, you will agree again with the psalmist in Psalm 119, when he says, 'It is good for me that I have been afflicted; that I might learn thy statutes' (verse 71).

God's faithfulness

If in all things you give thanks to God, always, whatever is happening, you will find yourself led to this final conclusion: you can always be confident in God. Looking back across his life, David says, 'I have been young, and now am old; yet have I not seen the righteous forsaken, nor his seed begging bread' (Psalm 37:25).

If you are a child of God, he will never let you go. He will perfect that which he has purposed concerning you. Yes, he may chastise you; he will chisel corners off you; he will knock bits off you. He would have you conform to the image of his dear Son, and, as you realise it is happening to you, though it is painful at the moment (as the author of the epistle to the Hebrews puts it in that twelfth chapter), you know that afterwards it will yield 'the peaceable fruit of righteousness' (Hebrews 12:11). So when you are full of aches and pains, and are being pummelled in the gymnasium of God, you are thanking him. Thanking him! And, in a sense, you say, 'Go on with it, make me what you would have me to be.'

'In the name of our Lord Jesus Christ'

And, lastly, thanks are to be given 'in the name of our Lord Jesus Christ'. Why? Because you cannot approach God except in the name of the Lord Jesus Christ. It is through him that all the blessings come to us, but, above all, it is through him that we become children of God.

God is God to everybody, as we have seen. He is the God of the universe. Yes, but Paul says, 'Giving thanks always for all things unto God and *the Father*'. And God is my Father because, first of all, he is the God and Father of our Lord and Saviour Jesus Christ.

'But', you say, 'he is Christ's Father, so where do I come in?' You have been put into Christ, and because you are in him, God is your Father also. He is not your Father apart from Christ. It is in Christ that you are saved. It is in Christ that you receive adoption. So you say, 'God has made me his child, and I have become a member of the very household of God.'

Oh, the apostle never can leave out the name of Christ. He has been repeating this name right through the epistle. Whether you pray, whether you give thanks, whatever it is, it must always be in the name of our Lord Jesus Christ.

Give thanks!

Shame on us, Christian people, that we ask so much and thank so little, that we are so ready to grumble and so slow to praise! Our need is the need of being filled with the Spirit, because when we are filled with him, he does enlighten us and open the eyes of our understanding. Then we know 'what is the hope of his calling, and what the riches of the glory of his inheritance in the saints, and what is the exceeding greatness of his power to us-ward who believe' (Ephesians 1:18-19).

The Holy Spirit will lead us to the Scriptures, to meditation, to consideration. And as we realise these things, our hearts will be bursting with a desire to thank and to praise God: 'Giving thanks always for all things unto God and the Father in the name of our Lord Jesus Christ.'

Out of the Depths
Studies in Psalm 51

Repentance is a subject which no one can afford to ignore. It is impossible for a person to become a Christian without it. Repentance is also a continuing and indispensable part of the Christian's experience throughout his life on earth. He sins daily, and he must therefore daily repent. Without repentance he will know nothing of salvation, holiness or real joy in the Christian life.

But what exactly is repentance and what does it involve? How can I be sure that I have experienced *real* repentance and not some counterfeit version of it? How can I be a truly happy Christian?

In this moving study of Psalm 51, Dr Lloyd-Jones examines these and similar questions in a sensitive, spiritual and compassionate manner. Earnest seekers, troubled Christians and all those involved in counselling them will find plenty of help in this masterly exposition. It is a veritable mine of practical application and pastoral wisdom.

It is a book which makes both humbling and exhilarating reading.

Bryntirion Press
Bryntirion, Bridgend,
CF31 4DX
Wales, UK

70 pp. ISBN 1 85049 036 8

True Happiness

An exposition of Psalm 1

Everywhere people seek happiness only to be dis-appointed in their search. This is because they seek it as an end in itself, whereas Dr Martyn Lloyd-Jones maintains it is only to be found in knowing God.

In this exposition of Psalm 1, originally preached as four New Year sermons at the beginning of 1963, Dr Lloyd-Jones shows the profound difference between true happiness and all false substitutes which people try to put in its place.

Bryntirion Press
Bryntirion, Bridgend,
CF31 4DX
Wales, UK

93 pp. ISBN 1 85049 138 0

Why does God allow war?

In this masterly series of sermons—preached in October 1939 only a few weeks after Britain had declared war on Nazi Germany—Dr Lloyd-Jones first addresses the larger question 'Why does God allow suffering?' He then moves on to the narrower question 'Why does God allow war?'

In a world full of suffering and plagued by wars this classic book (now completely reset) will help readers to think their way through to biblical answers and to experience Christian comfort.

Bryntirion Press
Bryntirion, Bridgend,
CF31 4DX
Wales, UK

109 pp ISBN 1 85049 023 6

Let everybody praise the Lord

An exposition of Psalm 107

As he expounds this wonderful psalm Dr Lloyd-Jones sees a great choir, drawn from the four corners of the earth, united in praising God. Using the Psalmist's vivid word-pictures he underlines the sheer grace of God who rescues sinners from the *wilderness,* frees them from *prison,* heals them from dreadful *disease,* and saves them from a terrible *storm.*

Throughout this superb exposition Dr Lloyd-Jones shows the profound difference between false and true religion. True Christianity always, and inevitably, leads to heart-felt praising of God 'for his goodness and for his wonderful works to the children of men' (verse 31).

Bryntirion Press
Bryntirion, Bridgend,
CF31 4DX
Wales, UK

151 pp ISBN 1 85049 164 X

Heirs of Salvation

Studies in biblical assurance

Christians are meant to know that they are sons of God; they are meant to have a full assurance of faith. But how can they obtain this assurance?

The author suggests that the best way to approach this question is to look at some examples of men and women of Scripture who have rejoiced in this assurance. To that end he leads us to the gallery of saints in Hebrews 11—Abel, Enoch, Abraham and Moses—men who triumphed because they were sure of their relationship to their Heavenly Father. He tells us that if we are lacking in assurance nothing is more profitable than to discover what brought them to this position of assurance.

In this series of sermons Dr Lloyd-Jones shows how we can banish all our dark misgivings and come to a position of clear Scriptural assurance.

Bryntirion Press
Bryntirion, Bridgend,
CF31 4DX
Wales, UK

100 pp ISBN 1 85049 174 7

Not Against Flesh and Blood

The battle against spiritual wickedness in high places

The Church and the Christian must always be aware that 'We wrestle not against flesh and blood, but against the rulers of the darkness of this world, against spiritual wickedness in high places' (Ephesians 6:12).

In these previously unpublished sermons, preached in November/December 1960 as part of a series on Christian Warfare, the author reminds us that the devil operates on a worldwide scale as well as upon individuals. He traces the confusion and chaos of present-day society to the destructive work of Satan and states that, in a day when there is renewed interest in the occult, spiritism and 'doctrines of devils', to be unaware of these evil powers will almost certainly mean that we are defeated by them.

Bryntirion Press
Bryntirion, Bridgend,
CF31 4DX
Wales, UK

77pp ISBN 1 85049 179 8

What is the Evangelical Movement of Wales?

The Evangelical Movement of Wales serves as a vehicle to promote the gospel of Jesus Christ in Wales.

The Movement is a fellowship of churches and individuals who accept the Holy Scriptures, as originally given, as the infallible Word of God, of divine inspiration. Recognising them as our sole authority in all matters of faith and practice.

What are the Movement's aims?
We believe that God raised up the Movement in the 1940s in order to serve both English and Welsh speakers. Therefore the Movement pursues the following aims in both languages:

Promoting the fundamental truths of the Christian faith and helping Christians to think and act biblically

Fostering evangelism, revival and godly living

Co-operating with like-minded bodies at home and abroad for the furtherance of the gospel

Assisting with the training and support of Christian workers and those aspiring to Christian service.

How does the Movement seek to achieve its aims?
The following are the main activities in which the Movement is engaged.

Undertaking evangelism in conjunction with local churches, through literature stands and witness teams at the Urdd and National Eisteddfodau and in collaboration with other bodies. Providing indoor and outdoor camps during school holidays annually for up to 1000 young people aged between 10 and 21.

Producing books, including the widely used hymn book, *Christian Hymns*, audio cassettes, evangelistic tracts and the Evangelical Magazine (English and Welsh) through Bryntirion Press and distributing these in Wales, the UK and overseas.

Maintaining a daily witness to the gospel and a resource centre for books, Sunday School materials etc, for the Christian community through its network of Christian Bookshops.

Providing a part-time Theological Training Course in English and Welsh for persons in full-time employment who aspire to the ministry or who wish to deepen their knowledge of the Christian faith. EMW also arranges ministers' fellowships and conferences for mutual encouragement and development.

Providing at the Bryn-y-groes Conference Centre, Bala comfortable residential facilities in a beautiful location for church groups, mature Christians, families, camps, conferences and retreats. Further information can be obtained from The Manager, Bryn-y-groes, Bala, Gwynedd, LL23 7YE.

Organising week long Conferences in English and Welsh for Bible teaching and fellowship each August at Aberystwyth, as well as occasional conferences, rallies, workshops, mornings of ministry and prayer times at other venues.

Seeking to promote a world wide vision of the Christian Church and awareness of opportunities for Christian service, through an Annual Missions Exhibition run in conjunction with the English Conference, and through articles and reports in its magazines. It also works through other organisations such as The Almond Tree Trust, Book Aid and Christian Books for Africa to send good Christian literature to needy church leaders overseas

Co-operating with other Christian organisations that share its convictions and aims. These include the Associating Evangelical

Churches of Wales, the Association of Christian Teachers of Wales, the Christian Council for the Schools of Wales, Go Teach, the Evangelical Theological College of Wales (with whom we share the Bryntirion site) as well as individual churches. EMW is also currently working with other evangelical organisations in the production of the first ever Welsh Study Bible.

Providing a facility through EMW Trust Ltd for the administration of tax efficient giving by individuals and churches by way of Gift Aid, and for acting as a custodian or holding trustee for churches.

How is the Movement funded?

The Movement is a registered charity whose main source of funding is its earned income. This comes from the shops, and charges made for activities such as camps and conferences, and from publications. Charges are kept as reasonable as possible to make sure people can afford to attend, but have to be sufficient to ensure that the Movement is able to maintain and develop the work and pay its staff honourably without incurring debts.

The second source of funding for the Movement is gift income. The generous and faithful giving of individuals and churches is vital in enabling the Movement to undertake evangelism and in supporting the evangelistic work of churches. Regular standing order giving is particularly helpful as it enables the Movement to plan its commitments. Furthermore, if gifts are also enhanced by Gift Aid, then they yield extra income through the recovery of income tax. It is also remarkable how often legacies have come at a time when some development is being contemplated and have proved a gracious provision of God for the work.

The Movement manages its finances on the basis that God will provide the resources necessary to complete the work undertaken at His bidding and in His way. When a gift is made to support a particular aspect of the work it is always designated in accordance with the giver's wishes.

Further information regarding any of these matters and a current programme of events can be obtained from the Movement's Bryntirion Office

Evangelical Movement of Wales
Bryntirion, Bridgend, CF31 4DX
Tel: 01656 655886 Fax: 01656 665919
Email: office@emw.org.uk
Website: www.emw.org.uk

Registered Charity No 222407